Copyright © 2025 by Brendan French.

All rights reserved.

No part of this publication may be reproduced, distributed, or transmitted in any form by any means, including photocopying, recording, or other electronic or mechanical methods.

Book cover by Charlotte Fleming.

Edited by Cordelia French.

1st Edition 2025.

This book is dedicated to Cordelia and Daniel French.

Sailors Tell Yarns

Introduction

I'm a raconteur. I grew up in South East London and was always visiting Dublin where characters in pubs told jokes and stories. A true story is far better than any joke. I was born lucky, surrounded by people who were funny, who could tell stories. This seems to be a dying art; it seems people now share funny things through social media. They share someone else's joke as though this makes them funny. What follows is a collection of my life stories, all true. They seem to amuse people, I hope they do you.

I am not a writer, although I love literature. I have tried to write as I speak, warts and all. As though I'm telling you a story in the pub. They're in no particular order or timeline.

Hope you like them.

All for Laurie Lee

~ I love the way he uses words, will it work as well for me

Sorry said the words; we only do it for Laurie Lee

But words are common property, they're available and free

Said the words, we're very choosey and we've chosen Laurie Lee

I want to write like he does, but the words did all agree

Sorry Son we're spoken for, we belong to Laurie Lee

~

- Roger McGough

1. Look in His Shoe
2. Uncle Willie
3. I Won't Get Laid Tonight
4. The Hokey Cokey
5. Four Generations
6. Brendan Behan
7. The Irish Grand National
8. Leonard Cohen
9. Tony the Dog
10. The Two Buckets
11. The Kings Cross Fire
12. Piss Fight at Mano's Roundabout
13. The Trapeze Artist
14. Stag Night
15. The Flannel
16. What a Four Ball
17. Bits of Prose
18. Marvin Hagler
19. Benidorm
20. Beautiful Asian Eyes
21. Leaving Home
22. Letters of thanks
23. Throw Her on the Couch
24. The Snip
25. How My Kids Got Their Names
26. A Narcissist
27. Amnesty International
28. The Tree Hugging Course
29. Heaven and Hell

30. Uncle Miles
31. My Mum
32. Another Crane Story
33. Dogs
34. Neil Whinstone
35. IVF
36. The Marchioness
37. Irish Instructions
38. God Needs a Dentist
39. Rolf Harris
40. Arse
41. Mediterranean Mooring
42. Nigel Farage
43. Foxes

Look in His Shoe

I'm in bed fast asleep, must have been about ten years old, after midnight. My old man comes in, pissed as a newt and sits on the end of my bed. He would do this quite often when drunk and basically brag about himself. What a hard man he was, or when I got older everyone would tell me what a great man he was. I was his captive audience, smelling his beer-stained breath and hoping my mum would come in and rescue me.

Anyway, he takes off his shoe and his feet stink of sweat. He then pulls a load of pound notes out of his shoe and starts bragging that he's worth loads of money. I was only a kid but knew somehow that this is deceitful. He then makes me give him my word that I wouldn't say anything about it to my mum. He finally leaves and I fall asleep, glad he's gone.

I come home from school the next day and my mum is sitting around the kitchen table and there are bills spread all about the place. And small piles of money made up of shillings and tanners etc, obviously this is pre-decimal. But she is getting agitated because she can't make all the money go round to pay everything. I could see the worry in her face.

Later that night in my old man comes in pissed as a newt again; face all red, runny nose and wet eyes, a typical drunk. My mum, who was obviously stressed and knew he was out on the piss, went for him straight away. She had him by the scruff of the neck and was punching him in the face, saying, "Where's the fucking money? I've to feed the children. Where's the fucking money?" which always has more meaning if delivered in a strong Irish accent.

I jumped up and started kicking him to help my mum, I was only a child and had little slippers on, but I had to help her. I'd seen her almost in tears counting the money, or lack of it, in the kitchen. But the worst part of it was I knew he had money in his shoe, but I was sworn to secrecy and some misguided moral compass told me not to say anything. But in my head, I'm screaming out, "Look in his shoe mum, look in his shoe".

~ This snail gets mugged by a tortoise. The police are called. The policeman says, "In your own words Mr Snail tell me exactly what happened" and the snail says, "Well it all happened so fast I can't really remember." ~

Uncle Willie

Every year my mum would take my sister and me to Ireland. To Crumlin, Dublin, for our holidays. This would be for a month or the majority of the summer holidays. It was never called going on holiday, it was called going home.

All my uncles and aunties were really good to me; they all took us for days out. Everywhere from Dublin Zoo to pinkeen fishing on the canals, up the Dublin Mountains, or to the seaside. But I remember one particular time my Uncle Willie taking us to Bray, Dublin's beach.

Now what was special about this trip was Willie had a Morris Minor car, black in colour and red leather seats. It was a fairly small car but I have great memories of it. He had his wife, Collette, sat next to him and my mum and her sisters, my Auntie Pat and Auntie Betty, in the back seats, so the car was pretty full up. But they were all good Irish Catholic girls, every sperm was sacred. My Auntie Pat had four kids, Collette had four kids, Betty had two and my mum had two. That's twelve of us cousins in the car. There were kids everywhere, on the floor on every lap, on the back shelf. Some tied to the roof. The older kids had to run behind the car, but they were always glad of the lift!

It was chaos in this car, kids screaming, nappies needed changing and this was before disposable nappies, absolute chaos. And then my Uncle Willie would have a good idea. He would stop and buy everyone an ice cream. That's seventeen ice creams. Now it just got worse. There's ice cream running down the windows, ice cream on the floor. It was so packed in the car that my Auntie Pat was holding her ice cream so close to her chest it fell down her top. That was the happiest I'd seen my Auntie Pat until the Pope said a mass at Phoenix Park. And every child had a mouth covered in ice cream, smothered in it. But that didn't matter because every Irish mother always had a Kleenex up every sleeve to wipe a dirty mouth or to wipe away a tear.

So now I can't tell you how crazy it was in this car, you'd be arrested for it now, twelve minors in a car and not one of them strapped in. But it was a different time; this must have been about '69, '70. Anyway, no matter how much chaos was happening in the car my Uncle Willie was just so happy. Now when an Irishman is happy he breaks into song, he can't help himself, it's in the blood, which is probably why I keep doing it. Willie would always sing the same song, and he was good at it, and the song was 'A White Sport Coat and a Pink Carnation'.

He died right in the middle of the first Covid outbreak so I couldn't go 'home' to say goodbye.

I loved him but I don't know why. When I was a kid all he ever done was tell me off. He'd point his finger at me and say, "Come here you, I want a word with you. You don't be upsetting your mammy." He was a great husband, a great father, a great brother and to me a great uncle.

~ A white sport coat and a pink carnation

I'm all dressed up for the dance

A white sport coat and a pink carnation

I'm in the mood for romance. ~

I Won't Get Laid Tonight

It's Friday night, I'm still living at home, and I've pulled. She was gorgeous and I'm taking her up to my bedroom. As we get to the front door of the council flat I lived in, I heard this screaming and shouting I'd heard a thousand times before. My old man is as pissed as a newt, and my mum is beating the shit out of him. Outside our front door there are iron banisters in the communal hallway. The old man is on the floor covered in blood, screaming for help, my mum is punching him in the face as hard as she can, the same old story, "Where's the fucking money?"

This girl is in shock. Obviously, she had never seen anything like this before. She is trying to calm my mum down and has got a flannel from the bathroom and is wiping the blood from my dad's face. My mum is shouting out, "Don't be helping that bastard" and the old man is shouting out, "Get the police". And I'm thinking same old Friday night, they will have made up by Wednesday. It was a regular occurrence. I grew up with it.

After a while it all calms down, but it has really affected this girl, she's shaking, totally in shock. And I think to myself, I won't get laid tonight. So, I say, "I'm sorry you had to see that, come on I'll take you home".

~ Sex without love is an empty experience, but as 'empty experiences' go, it ain't bad. ~

The Hokey Cokey

We start a new tour of duty at Euston Fire Station. After roll call and a quick cup of tea we were ordered to carry out inventories. No one got excited about this task; it was just necessary. A firefighter is no use without his equipment. So, because we all haven't seen each other for four days, everyone is chatting, what they had been up to.

Our leader, our station officer, is Station Officer McKenzie. He was very insecure in himself, and this led to unnecessary behaviour. He was very much the same sort of character as Mr Mackie in 'Porridge'. And certainly wasn't of supreme intellect. So, on this day he walked around the corner and because we were all chatting, he barks out, "Get on with your work you lazy bastards". Everyone was kind of in shock, it was just unnecessary.

So I said, "We're not being lazy Guvnor, we're trying to work out how to do the Hokey Cokey", "I mean when do you put your left leg in? When the right? When do you turn around? And what is the Hokey Cokey?"

So he stands in the middle of us and says, "Get out of the way" and our leader, our station officer, does the whole Hokey Cokey, the left leg, the right leg, even running back and forward in the circle that had now come around him. And he ends on the big stage show ending with his hands outstretched.

So we're standing there looking at him and he pulls his shoulders back, sticks his chin out and mutters to himself, "Showed them bastards". So I went up to him, put my arm on his shoulder and said, "Thanks Guv, it's appreciated, thank you." And he walked away. We just fell about laughing, all of us in stitches. I will never forget Richard Lockwood saying to me, "What just happened?"

~ Mind you, I can't be too hard on him, I was addicted to the Hokey Cokey once, but I've turned myself around and that's what it's all about! ~

Four Generations

When my sister Sandra had her first child, Amy, they were going 'home' to see my grandmother, Mummy Hollowed as we all called her, and she was delighted. She was telling everyone that there would be four generations in the house this Whitsun. Everyone in the shops in Crumlin knew this great news. She was so proud.

And then a week before they were due to go, she died, unexpectedly, all of a sudden. And this was devastating news. So, everyone that thought they were going for a celebration was now going for a funeral.

My old man and me, who weren't meant to be going, ended up getting the ferry over. This all had to be done in a hurry as they bury them very quickly in Ireland.

I remember being very trepidatious turning up and knocking on the door, the door I had knocked so many times before and getting a warm loving welcome. But what happened was a shock to me. The door opened and whoosh I got hit by this atmosphere, everyone was drinking and laughing, it was one of the best social events I have ever attended. Old fashioned Irish wakes are amongst the most amazing, special things you can go too.

Anyway, we went to the funeral, something I've never liked and don't see the point of. I don't want one, get rid of the body and I hope the people that care about me all get pissed at the Turf Hotel.

After that we went to the graveyard and they put her in a hole in the ground, it was awful. When the priest had done his duty and most of the congregation had left, I was standing next to my mum. My sister was holding Amy in her arms, and I heard my mum say very quietly, "There's four generations here now Ma."

~ Crossed the water, on a ferry

Back to Ma's house, with my daddy

There's four generations here now Ma

Down in the old town, she told the story

Come this Whitsun, they'd make history

By having four generations here now Ma

Went to the graveyard, one of them lying

Three of them standing, three of them crying

There's four generations here now Ma. ~

Brendan Behan

Amongst my personal heroes are Nelson Mandela, Che Guevara, Martin Luther King, Gerry Adams and my namesake Brendan Behan. All were considered criminals at one time but ended up being heroes to millions.

My mum's brother Miles's best friend when growing up in Dublin was Brendan Behan. If you don't know who he was, he was the unofficial spokesperson for the IRA in the sixties. He's also an author of repute. Look him up on YouTube; they would always have him on late night discussion shows, and they would bring in some professors to try and make him look a fool, but he was always too smart for them.

The last time I was in Ireland with my mum I asked her if she remembered where Brendan lived and she said, "Course she did". I asked if she could show me and we walked up to his house. It was round the corner from my grandmother's, and there was a blue plaque outside, the same we have in England, to note a famous person lived there once. I got a photo taken outside the house and we walked back.

On the way I asked her if she remembered him. She said, "Brendan. Of course I remember Brendan, he was always around the house". And then I said,

"What was he like"? Now in my head I'm thinking this is the same as a little child in South Africa, who grew up around Nelson Mandela. I'm going to get an insight into an IRA spokesperson from the sixties. I will never forget her response, "Ah he was always talking politics, you know one of those fecking ejits!"

If you think about it, it's one of the most intelligent answers you could give. It's the fore runner of the Good Friday Agreement. Stop talking politics and start talking peace. How many times have you heard an uneducated person make the most sense?

My favourite Brendan Behan story...

~ In 1916 the IRA or Irish Citizen Army as it was then, seized the General Post Office in O'Connell Street, Dublin. The British soldiers were shelling it from all angles to gain back control.

There was a lull in the fighting and when the smoke cleared there was a little Irish voice could be heard, "Paddy? Are you up there Paddy?"

Paddy says, "Bridey, go home, you'll be killed go home".

Bridey shouts back, "Tell me Paddy, how long will you be up there? Will I do your sandwiches for your work in the morning?"

Paddy shouts back, "I'm staying here till the fucking Brits get out of my country, now go home Bridey you'll be killed, go home".

So, Bridey shouts back, "Well Paddy throw us a few postage stamps down and I'll be on me way"! ~

The Irish Grand National

I've got a relation in Ireland called 'Cuts Mooney' a second cousin I think and I don't know his real name. He got the nickname because when he was a kid, he was always cutting his knees in his short trousers. And he was wild. He was the wildest child I had ever come across and I loved it, being with him was the best craic ever. 'Cuts' would get me to say I was staying over with him and he'd tell his mum he was staying over with me and we'd go out in Dublin all night and just get up to the maddest stuff ever, most of it not quite legal. We must have been about twelve or thirteen. I remember one night we broke into a Jameson Whiskey depot and stole a crate of whiskey and were drinking it in the park at night. I was pissed and getting so sick that what looked like lumps of marshmallow were pouring out of my throat. In the end a load of older boys came along, beat the shit out of us and stole our stolen whiskey.

Another time, later, probably about sixteen, I was in a pub with 'Cuts' and his brother Rory. Now at that time, at closing time, the pubs in Dublin would play 'Danny Boy' or 'Fields of Athenry' and everyone would stand to attention, and a collection would be held for the IRA. I was just a kid and I'm full up with larger bubbles and I'm pissed, and I've got an English accent. I found the whole thing funny and got the giggles. I went to have a slash and got pushed up against a toilet wall and a knife stuck in my throat. This was being pushed so hard I could feel a trickle of blood running down my neck and I shit myself. Fortunately, Rory had seen the two boys follow me into the toilet and comes in, "Leave him alone, he's a Hollowed". The two boys say, "He's a Hollowed? Well he should know fucking better". And they leave and I'm thinking thank fuck I'm a Hollowed. Thank fuck I'm a Hollowed!

But the story I want to tell is this. All around Dublin are council estates, they're called corporation housing in Ireland. Most of my family lived in such places. All of these estates had open grass areas for the kids to play, and I presume the planners had tried to design a better living space for its inhabitants. But this is Ireland and most of them had a small family of Gypsies living on them. We refer to them as Pikeys in England, in Ireland they're known as Knackers. They're not English and they're not Irish. They don't speak English and they don't speak Irish. They're their own culture and fascinating.

Anyway, in their little camp would be a couple of caravans, horse drawn, an old van, about four adults, two or three horses, and loads of kids and a big fire right in the middle of the camp.

Me and 'Cuts' are walking past one late at night and he puts his finger to his lips, and we walk up to it. Before I know what is happening he throws me up on this horse, he jumps on another one and he shouts, "GET UP". The two horses start running down the road. He could ride a horse; he was sat upright holding this nag's mane and making it run faster. I'm just clinging onto my nag's neck as tight as I could, just trying not to fall off.

The Knackers have heard us and are chasing after us with knives and sticks. I am shitting myself, I'm clinging on for dear life, and I'm being chased by a load of armed Knackers. It was only an old cart horse, but to me it was going so fast, I literally thought I was in the Grand National.

Anyway, we got away. We jumped off the horses, they just ran back to where they come from and me and 'Cuts' were laughing our heads off.

~ Two cannibals are eating a clown, and one says to the other, "Does this taste funny to you?" ~

Lenard Cohen

Spetses is a beautiful island. I love the Greek Islands; they are simply the best place to take a holiday. I know I'm right because Martin told me. Martin Potter is an old friend, he spent the best part of ten years travelling the world, there is nowhere he hasn't been. Mongolia, South America, Middle East, everywhere. I asked him once, "Where's the best place to go on holiday? He said, "If you want a holiday, the perfect place to go is Greece". I've always agreed with that. There are other places you must go, but for a holiday it's the Greek Islands.

Spetses is the island John Fowels uses as the location for 'The Magus'. A fascinating book, read it, his best, better than 'The French Lieutenant's Women'.

I went there for the first time with Alison, my daughter Chloe's mum. We were in love then. I had a great year with her and then spent fifteen years arguing. C'est la vie.

I was telling Stan we were going there and he gave me a tape to listen to. It was all Walkmans then not phones. The tape was Lenard Cohen. If you've known his music, you will know it's different, most people think it's depressing and dismiss it. That was my first thought. But when you listen, get into it, it's amongst the most moving music you can hear. Layer upon layer of different emotion. Every song is three dimensional. One song, 'Famous Blue Raincoat' is about a married man whose marriage has hit rock bottom. His brother comes to stay and fucks his wife. The song takes the form of a letter he sends to his brother thanking him for what he had done. He made him realise how special his wife is. He had forgotten. But the honesty in the song about his jealously is so profound.

Anyway, back to Spetses. I'm on a ferry for a day trip to Hydra, a little island just off Spetses and I'm listening to this tape. There's one song 'So Long Marianne'. The song is driving me nuts trying to work out what the lyrics mean, the story is so intriguing. It's in my head all day, more than the normal thing where you just whistle the tune a few times. This song has become a part of me. I'm absorbed by it. It's moved me like a painting can or a great book.

I was having lunch in the harbour. Alison is walking around the shops they put there to get some money out of tourists. That's fair enough but pointless. I'm sitting outside this cafe smoking, drinking coffee. Thank God for caffeine, nicotine and pavement cafés.

I'm sitting there and as I'm listening to the song, something is happening to me that I can't explain. I'm having an experience, like someone has walked over my grave. I don't know what it is, it's just happening. It freaks me out and I leave.

When I get home Stan asks me about the tape. I tell him I liked it, especially the song 'So Long Marianne' and he gives me a video tape.

The video is a documentary following Lenard Cohen on a concert tour. He plays in Hydra. He's on the same ferry as me going to the same island. He's standing on the same part of the boat I was standing when I first heard the song. He's now sitting in the same café; in exactly the same chair explaining what the song is all about, when I was trying to work out what this song is all about. I'm shivering with the whole spookiness of this. There are too many coincidences for it to be a coincidence. It's like a trip in time, we're both doing the same thing just at different times.

It affected me. I believe in coincidences, or I mean I don't, there is no such thing. Coincidences happen for a reason, they point you in a direction. Think about your life, all the major things happened because of a coincidence. I would like to think there is some great big cosmic being controlling us, God, but I don't think that is true. I just know coincidences happen for a reason.

By the way if you're interested, the song is about Lenard Cohen living on Hydra with Marianne. They spend ten years together on the island but at the end of this time they had to part and move on. They are still in love, but that caring love, it's over.

~ So long Marianne, it's time that we began

To laugh and cry and laugh and laugh about it all again ~

Tony the Dog

I'm over the park Sunday afternoon with my dog, Tony, and there was a restaurant called *La Mason* that backed onto the park. There was a brick wall that separated the park from the restaurant, and this was easy to climb over. A load of older boys had broken into the restaurant and was stealing the cash that had been left in the till and all the beers and wines. I was only about ten or eleven, so I had no interest in alcohol but all us younger kids was also in the restaurant because it was so exciting to break in. The only thing I found worth stealing was a waiters' jacket and a bow tie. So I took them and put them on Tony the Dog. The dog is now running around the park in the waiters' jacket and bow tie, it was hilarious, even the dog was excited and knew it was funny.

So the older boys are getting pissed and everyone is having a good laugh at the dog. All of a sudden the police are at the entrance to the park and everyone ran. The good thing about that park was there were so many exits, over garden fences, or into the builder's yard, you could just get out in a hurry. Everyone knew them and everyone got away. There's only Tony the Dog running around the park with his address on his collar. The police obviously caught him got the address and I was the only kid who got nicked.

I had to go to Bromley Police Station with my mother and father to receive a caution from the police sergeant.

My old man could never face anything like that sober; he just couldn't do it, he had to get pissed. So I turn up with my mum, and the old man turns up as pissed as a newt and we're taken into the sergeant's office. When my old man was drunk, he was always blurry eyed, face all red and a runny nose. And a drinker's pocket then was always full of change from buying beer.

So the three of us are standing in front of the sergeant, who is sat behind his desk, and my old man pulls out his hanky from his pocket to wipe his runny nose and a load of change goes all over the floor. The old man bends down to pick up all the change that is scattered all over the floor and every time he picks up a coin he says, "I'm sorry, Sir, I'm sorry Sir". In this broad Irish accent. He finally picks all the money up and goes to put it in his pocket, but because he's pissed, he misses his pocket, and the money goes all over the floor again and the, 'I'm sorry-ing' starts again.

I couldn't contain myself any longer and burst into laughter. The sergeant is fuming but realises there is no point going on with this farce any longer and orders me out of his office. And gives me one of those looks that says, 'You'll be back'.

~ As a foot note, Tony the Dog went mad, he had to be tied up next to my mum or he would attack people including us. All the violence in our house sent the poor mutt mad. I never knew if he ran away or he was put down. He just disappeared one day, and everyone said they didn't know what happened. ~

The Two Buckets

I was about nineteen, got a phone call that I had to ring my trainer, Richard Atkins. Got in touch, he told me I'm fighting tonight in Leeds so we would have to leave early to be there on time. I always hated it when this happened; I like to plan my training, roadwork, diet, sleep etc. Didn't like last minute preparation, it threw me out.

Anyway, got home early and told the old man what was happening and he said, "Can I come with you?" I said I'd ask Richard, and he said it was fine. There are three of us now in the car to Leeds, driving through the rush hour, it's dark and it's raining, just awful.

It seemed to take ages to get there, but just before we turned up Richard says to my dad, "Brendan, you'll have to work the corner with me". My old man was made up on this, delighted. Richard gave him a tabard with *Eltham A.B.C.* on the back and I caught him looking in the mirror with his tabard on. We parked up, got my bag with my kit in and Richard went off to get me booked in. He came back minutes later and said, "Hurry up Brendan, we're on first". I thought fuck this is all rush, rush.

Every time I fought, I had a routine I would go through. The main thing to do is to keep your nerves under control, your nerves will tire you out and you end up leaving all your strength and training in the changing room. Then find the changing room, get yourself comfortable, there will be a lot of other boys there all waiting to fight. Then have a big dump, your nerves will open your bowels up. You also have to see the doctor to make sure you're ok to fight. Then get changed, I was meticulous in my dress. I had blue velvet shorts with my name on. Boots as light as air and I'd take my time to lace up correctly. Take time in bandaging my hands, if done correctly with proper gauze bandage, when you make a fist your hand becomes solid. Then find out what time you're fighting and warm up at the start of the fight before you. This is proper stretching, every muscle in your body, just shadow boxing in the mirror is pointless. Always remembering to keep hold of your nerves.

Sometimes you would see your opponent. I always liked it when he was white with big muscles and tattoos, especially if he would try to stare you out. I would think to myself easy money. What was worse was if he was black, softly spoken and politely come over to shake your hand and wish you good luck. Then you would catch him getting changed, with a fantastic body, fit as fuck. And then think 'Fuck', this is going to hurt.

Anyway, none of this is happening, I'm just angry at having to rush. My son, Dan, would say, when I'm like this, "Dad is triggered". And my old man is pestering me as to what he has to do; I really didn't have time for him. But said "Dad there's two buckets, a clean and a dirty bucket. If Richard uses the sponge use the clean water, if I need to spit use the dirty bucket and don't mix them up". Sometimes if a fight is hard or the crowd is going wild, buckets get mixed up. You don't drink water in a fight, but you really want to, so you end up sucking it out of the sponge as you get wiped down. You can end up bringing up a lot of phlegm in a fight, especially if you have been hit hard in the nose, or your lip can be cut, or your nose is bleeding. You end up putting quite a lot of stuff in the dirty bucket. If they get mixed up, you go back to your corner and get wiped down with your own blood and snot. It is awful.

Anyway, we go to the ring and I see my dad with two buckets in his hands saying to himself, as only a Paddy can, "Clean bucket, dirty bucket".

All of a sudden, the bell rings and this fella comes charging over at me. Now a lot of fighters are told to 'Show him who the guvnor is straight away'. So they will come at you and hit you with a big right hand. This bloke is charging over and he's loading up, meaning he has pulled his right arm back and is going to throw it.

If this happens you either block it and pull back a bit or if you're confident enough, you lean in on your left leg and let it go over your right shoulder. You must get the timing perfect for this, or you'll end up helping him to knock you out. This also has the advantage now of exposing him to your punches. So, I lean in and whack the side of his body and then throw a perfect left hook to his chin and he goes down. I think that's handy and run to a neutral corner. Before I know what is happening, I hear, "Seven, Eight, Nine, Ten". The Ref bends down and takes his mouthpiece out and the fight is over. Go back to my corner and Richard says, "That's handy; we can have an early night".

I look at my dad, and he is gutted. He knows he should be happy, but it's his first time to work a corner, he's finally got his head around the bucket set up and he hasn't had a chance to do any of it.

The three of us are back in the car to London; it seems we've only been out of the car for half an hour, and it took until Birmingham for that bastard to cheer up.

~ I wasn't good enough to turn professional, in fact I was the only fighter they ever had to carry into the ring. ~

The Kings Cross Fire

In 1987 I was serving at Euston Fire Station; I spent a total of eleven years there. We got the call to Kings Cross Underground on the way back from another call, so Soho Fire Station got there before us. I was driving that night and when I pulled up and jumped out Station Officer Townsley was lying on the floor, and the ambulance service was giving him shocks with a defibrillator. We knew then this was a serious fire.

When you're driving and you're not the first in attendance the first thing you do is help the other drivers set up, get a hose from a hydrant to their appliance. When all this was done, I was put in a crew of spare firefighters, all my crew had already been committed.

When we got down to the concourse, it was full of wooden shacks: tie racks, coffee stalls, etc.; all of them were alight. Also, the floor was covered in dead bodies, people lying around in all sorts of contorted positions. I think about forty people died that night, but it looked to me like hundreds lying on the floor and thought 'Jesus'. I had the hose and started to put the sheds out, the only way to do this was to kneel down in front of them and spray water over the counters. The heat had nowhere to escape to, so it was just getting hotter and hotter and knackering. Also, when a train came into the station, they hadn't stopped them yet, it caused a rush of hot air over you which burnt. The only way to protect yourself from this was that every hose nozzle, called branches, has a wheel you could turn, and a vertical spray comes out the side, like a mist to protect you. So, we would put our wrist and ears into the mist every time a train came.

After a while, the sub officer who was in charge of our crew noticed that the hose coming down the stairs had reignited and ordered us to back to secure our exit. At this point it crossed my mind that we could die down here. But we managed to put our way out, out.

All of a sudden, a firefighter from another crew stands up and presses his personal safety alarm; he was obviously suffering from heat stress. As soon as the sub officer sees him, he says to me "Get him out of here". This was music to my ears; I thought I can't wait to get the fuck out of here. I was knackered anyway from working the hose and dragged him up the stairs. This last part can all be seen on YouTube.

When the other firefighters grabbed him at the top of the stairs, I collapsed against some railings, and a wall of press started to take my photo, I remember telling them to, "Fuck off" and this went out on the ten o'clock news. They edited the 'Fuck off' out later. But my mum saw this and said to my dad, "That's Brendan".

What happened next was one of the most harrowing things I ever experienced in the London Fire Service.

When you go into a fire in breathing apparatus, you hand a tally in with your name and the time you entered. This is all coordinated by a firefighter and he is known as the control officer. On this night it was Roger Kendal. Roger had told the officer in charge that firefighters had not come out in time and would be running out of air, so an emergency roll call was called. I will never forget hearing Roger call out people's names, watch members, my mates, and they didn't answer. How Roger got through it is a miracle, but he was a general that night. Anyway, if you had been down there you knew you couldn't survive without air, so they were dead. We had already witnessed one firefighter, Station Officer Townsley, die in front of us. So now more had died.

People often ask me how I felt right then, but if you want to know the truth, I wanted to jump up, punch the air and shout, "Yes, I got out". Don't know if I should feel guilty about this but that is what happened.

So anyway, we had to rerig and go down and look for dead firefighters. Can you imagine that! As it turned out, they had dived down the platforms to get below the fire and were all ok. When we found them, it was so good, but they were just moaning like fuck saying, "What took you so long?".

Afterwards it became a circus, press frenzy, councillors and politicians trying to make gain out of it, firefighters lying about what they had done, apparently this is a common phenomenon. I pulled out of all the mayhem completely. Didn't go to Station Officer Townsley's Funeral and didn't talk about it much at the time because of all the lies.

My Kings Cross Tale.

~ I've got a four-year-old nephew, and he's just come back from his holiday in Spain, and he doesn't know how to say please in Spanish. That's poor for four isn't it. ~

Piss Fight at Mano's Roundabout

I'm in Magaluf, Mallorca. I'm about thirty years old. Boy's holiday, I went every year for a while, with a bunch of old reprobates. Stan, Richard, Ernie, Neil, and Warren, about thirty of us in all. The craic was great.

We would start and end every night in a bar called Mano's. This bar then was Sodom and Gomorrah. Every nut case in the world seemed to turn up there at some point. One night Warren was walking home after leaving the bar and noticed a big fat girl taking a piss up an alleyway and shouts at her, "Oh you dirty bitch". The girl starts pissing in a glass and chases Warren. Mano's was situated on a roundabout with a big monument in the middle and Warren is running around the monument to get away from being covered in piss. The girl is shouting at him and trying to get near enough to throw the piss over him. The pair of them were overweight, so this is the most comical scene you will ever witness.

One thing that made these holidays really good was a friend, Mickey Lynch, (known as The Colonel) would organise a theme every year. He put a lot of effort into this, and we all got a lot out of it. So, the next year's theme was to 'Commemorate the Piss Fight at Mano's Roundabout' and we were all invited to a veteran's dinner. Halfway through the meal, The Colonel pulls out a load of red berets, and there are now twenty of us sitting down to dinner looking like a load of ex-squaddies.

After the meal The Colonel lines us up outside the restaurant and orders us to, "Fall In", "By the Left, Quick March". What was funny was all of us knew how to march. Most of the guys were older and had done National Service. Stan was in the Boys' Brigade; I was a firefighter. So we all looked professional. Also, someone had nicked a flag off the golf course, and we marched behind this banner. The Colonel constantly barking out orders, "Eyes Forward" as we marched past a pretty girl or, "Stay in line, laddie" if someone wasn't marching properly. We were all a bit pissed, and it just seemed hilarious.

Anyway, we march down to Mano's roundabout but as we got there the most surreal thing happened. The police, seeing us coming stopped all the traffic. All the bars turned their music off. An eerie silence descended around the roundabout; little old ladies came out and stood in the street. And all of us thought 'Fuck' this isn't funny anymore. This monument obviously means something to them. To commemorate the fallen dead or something and we're just about to insult them. No one understood this more than The Colonel; he just got it and went completely professional. I remember thinking 'Well done, Mickey'.

The Colonel lined us up in front of the monument and called us to attention. We all, in time together, obeyed. And Stan, who, as mentioned was in the Boy's Brigade and could play the bugle, was ordered to take one pace forward to play 'The Last Post'. Stan was shitting himself, shaking, but played it beautifully. Not perfect, just with real emotion. Listening to it in the still quiet night was moving. And all the Majorcan's thought so too. It was a magical moment. Then The Colonel orders three cheers, this we do, and we all throw our berets in the air. The Majorcans come over to us and start to shake our hands, embracing us, some with a tear in their eye.

It was a really special moment and all because some fat bird had chased Warren around the roundabout with a pint of piss.

~ All ways sin a little or Jesus died for nothing. ~

The Trapeze Artist

Euston Fire Station, about 1986, we get a call to a crane driver, possible heart attack, stuck in a crane, British Library. We were the first to attend and I, and another couple of firefighters, begin to climb the crane. This was when the library was being built and the cranes were really tall, I mean really tall. We had to ascend a Jacob's Ladder; this is a metal ladder with a cadge around it to make it safer for you. We finally reach the top and there's a really huge, overweight, crane driver as dead as a dodo sitting in his cab.

We now had to get him down, but we were trying to figure out how to do this. We couldn't work out how he got up there, through the Jacob's Ladder, which was quite tight, and we would never be able to lower him down it. A dead body can be a nightmare to move.

Then somebody came up with the idea that we should lower him down with the crane. This seemed the obvious answer, and we set about doing this. I had to tie the rope on his feet, and we would hook this to the hook on the crane. I have never tied a knot so tight. It wasn't going to be my fault if he should slip out. So, we set it all up with his feet sticking out the cab, hooked onto the crane ready to be lowered.

Now the controls of a crane are very easy to operate. There are six buttons. Up, Down, In, Out, and Left or Right. All of you can drive a crane, but the skill is to press the buttons one push at a time, it's called pinching. If you hold down a button for a long time you lose control of the thing being lifted and it will start to swing. This can be very dangerous with a heavy weight on, like wet concrete.

I had been a crane driver on a building site when I was a kid. A concrete floor has to be poured in one whole slab, and all dry at the same time. If it was a long pour that was going to go over five o'clock, and the proper crane driver wanted to go home, I would get overtime to stay and do it. You couldn't get away with that now.

I don't know why but another firefighter had the controls, and he's pressed the 'out' button too hard and this crane driver went shooting out of the cab at what seemed like a hundred miles an hour. When he finally let go of the button he stopped immediately, and this poor bastard is swinging upside down on the end of the crane. He then starts letting him down but this increases the swinging, and there's this great big fat bloke swinging in the air and every one can see him from the ground.

Then there's a call on our radio, it's from our governor, the officer in charge, I don't know who it was, "Stop him fucking swinging". The poor bastard on the controls starts panicking and starts pressing buttons to try and stop him swinging, but he's just making it worse. At one point the fat bastard nearly hit the crane.

So we are looking at this dead body swinging over London. He looked like a trapeze artist, and all we can hear on the radio is, "Get him fucking down". We are now laughing so much; it was one of the funniest moments I have ever been involved with.

When we finally got him down to the ground, Greg Cox, a firefighter from London Euston came running over to the body. He knows this is going to be the 'press' shot. He was always getting his ugly mush in the papers or on television. But when he goes up to him, the contents of this crane driver's stomach emptied out all over Greg Cox. You could see it splash all over his back. We could see it from up in the crane. This finished us off; I was laughing so much I don't know how I got down off the crane.

~ I enjoyed my time in the fire brigade, but the best job I ever had was as a photographer's assistant, I used to rub the ice cubes on Page Three girls' nipples. ~

Stag Night

I went with Neil, who was my best man, to look at a couple of venues for my stag night, but in the end, we just decided on the 'Change of Horses' in Farnborough Village, which was my local. It was just easier. What was good about this venue was everybody turned up, the pub was packed, which always makes you feel good.

I knew Neil would get a strippergram; they were all the rage then; it was expected of him. So, as I knew this was going to happen, I asked Sarah, my future bride, to lend me her stockings, suspender belt, and a G-string. I put them on and went on my stag night.

Sure enough, about ten o'clock, in walks a woman police officer looking for Mr Brendan French. She takes off her cap, tussles her hair and starts to tell me what a 'naughty boy' I have been and that she was going to have to arrest me. She duly handcuffs my hands behind my back and seductively pulls my trousers around my ankles. The whole pub fell about laughing. I'm standing there, handcuffed with my trousers down in stockings and suspenders and a G-string. Everyone was absolutely pissing themselves and I'm just standing there saying, "What's up?", "What's the matter?". The strippergram girl shits herself; she didn't know what to do next and just takes off my hand cuffs and leaves the pub. And everyone just kept coming up to me saying, "I can't believe I've been talking to you all night, and you were standing there in women's underwear".

~ Exit Signs, they're on the way out. ~

The Flannel

A flannel is a piece of towelling cloth about eight inches square, normally of bright colour, an essential piece of paraphernalia for any bathroom, but less so in recent times. Its main purpose is to be soaped up with a bar of soap; this is achieved by rubbing the soap on the flannel, and it is now ready to be rubbed all over your body, 'all over'. Years ago, in most houses the flannel was shared by all members of the household. Because we now pay more attention to hygiene a flannel is very rarely shared, or not used at all.

My mother told me when she was a young girl growing up in Dublin, bath night was Sunday night. She had three brothers and four sisters, and her mother, father, and my mum all shared the same bathwater. That's ten people sharing the same bathwater. This bath was a galvanised tub brought in from the back yard and filled up with boiling water from a big old gas oven in the kitchen. All her family used newspaper as toilet paper all week, then shared the same water, and then, here's the thing, shared the same flannel. That flannel, if it could be analysed in a laboratory at the end of bath night would be, condemned.... The nicest word I can think of. My mum's family and indeed mine were not dirty and they were not unusual; the same thing was happening in every street in Dublin and in every working-class street in England. That's how they lived. I'm so thankful that by the time I came along in 1962 we had a designated separate bathroom, and all ran a clean bath for each person. We all still shared the same flannel though.

I remember once my mum telling me when she was about sixteen, she would get up for work, cycle ten miles to a box factory, sweat all day at work, cycle home, and then go dancing every night to Elvis and Bill Hayley. And bath once a week. She said, "We must have stunk" but so did everybody else.

I never use a flannel, I think they're disgusting. But I noticed when my son Dan came to stay with me in the lockdown, he would leave his own flannel in the shower.

The last time my mum came to stay with me here, dementia was severely taking over her life, so I had to wash her. She was also very dodgy on her feet and the only way I could wash her was to back her into the shower holding the back of a chair for stability. I was fine washing her hair and soaping her body under the copious amounts of water. But washing her private parts was something I couldn't do, I don't think a son should, it was a step too far. So, I grabbed Dan's flannel, covered it in shampoo and slowly got her to wash herself there. This took a lot of persuasion, and she kept trying to wash the chair because of her advanced dementia. Got her dry, she smelt lovely, in her night clothes and to bed. The same way she would have done for me all those years ago. And I slung the flannel.

Afterwards I smoked ten fags. I found the whole thing too stressful and realised I couldn't have her with me full time. I couldn't cope.

You must always try and get a smile from every situation; it's the only thing that matters. So when my son came down I told about washing my mum. But said don't worry about your flannel I've given it a good rinse and it's ok now. His response was indignation, disgust, shock and that he didn't want to use the flannel. I could not stop laughing.

> ~ Mark Twain sat down in the barber's chair and was asked, "How do you want your hair cut?" … "In silence," said Mark Twain. ~

What a Four Ball

"What a four ball" that's what Stan said about Roger, Warren and me going to Greece. The four of us had decided to go to Faliraki, a town in Rhodes. According to Warren it was the place to be that season. We agreed to go with his recommendation because he was still young and trendy or at least knew what was. So, when Stan heard about the trip, he uttered the quip that always makes me smile, "Put me in".

I must tell you about our four ball, or five as it was now. There's Roger, he's fifty-two going on twenty-five. That says it all really. His best feature is that he tries to live life to the full. Stan, fifty-two, loves animals and children. Everybody likes Stan. Warren, twenty-eight, overweight, for some reason that fact becomes his main persona. Good fun, see what I mean. Laurence, also twenty-eight. Roger's nephew, cautious, loves a laugh. And me, thirty-two.

It felt a strange crowd, the five of us, as we touched down in Rhodes Airport. But, as always, there was two gorgeous girls waiting right next to us at the luggage collection. No matter where you go in the world there are always good-looking women to break your heart and cast you off like an old pair of socks. Anyway, we wasted no time in talking to them. They, as well as we, expected it. Roll on the obvious questions, "Where do you come from?", "Where are you staying?" Their faces dropped with pity when we said Faliraki. They said it was a hole, horrible, the worst place on the island. We just smiled and gave an arrogant look. We'll have a good time no matter where they put us. But deep down we were thinking, 'Shit, why did we listen to Warren?' We said goodbye to the girls. They said if you don't like Faliraki come and visit them in Lindos. "But how will we find you?" "Don't worry, you will. It's a small place, a beautiful small place".

There was a real buzz getting ready to go out that first night. Warren was ready by nine o'clock. I asked him why he was going out so early, "Northern birds get out early, and this place is full of northern birds" he said. This threw me. Was it true that the nearer the equator you went the later the girls go out? Come to think of it, it probably was. I've now got this vision of Eskimo girls going out the night before the disco starts.

Anyway, we walk into town with the aloofness of the characters in the opening scene of Reservoir Dogs. Done up in our pulling gear, full of pep and ginger. Nights like this are special; they make you feel so young. Even the older two felt it. Some lucky girl was going to get the best of me tonight if she wants it. The best chat, the best look, the best dance. All the best that I can offer. The gods can't let me go home alone tonight. But first we must eat.

We should have guessed right away that Faliraki was the wrong place to be when we couldn't find a decent restaurant. Eating out abroad is one of the joys of life, but every restaurant seemed to be a burger bar or some other 'and chips' affair. Eventually we settled on a sea front restaurant. Mainly for the view, not the food.

The food was crap, but that was now irrelevant because the town was ours. On the way to the 'strip' a group of buildings put together in the middle of nowhere, we passed a street attraction. A local Greek kid had made a goal out of old bits of wood and hung an old fishing net over it. His 'Evans' was put in goal, a small kid who stood there with his hands in his pockets. What made the attraction work was the delivery of the banter from the Greek kid. Anyone who had a slight resemblance to any famous footballer would be called over. If someone had blond curly hair he would shout, "Hey Shearer, three penalties one goal 500 Drachma, 50 Drachma a go". If he had red hair "Scholes". If he was black "Hey Pele" and so on. Everybody seemed to be delighted that they resembled some famous footballer and queued to have a go, all laughing as the next suspect was picked out, "Hey Beckenbauer".

All the other four had, at some time, played Sunday league football and could not resist the challenge. At that time Gascoigne was having trouble with his weight so inevitably Warren got called, "Hey Gascoigne, come on". What followed was one of the most embarrassing sights I have ever seen. No one could get one goal past the keeper. 'Evans' just stood there with his hands in his pockets side kicking the ball out of the goal. We watched for an hour or so, but no one could score. Admittedly the ball was not a perfect sphere, and the ground was rough. Just a piece of scrub that I would imagine has now got a hotel on it.

But the standard of penalty taking was abysmal. Young teenagers, who were obviously football fans, were incapable of sticking the ball cleanly. 'What chance have we got on the world stage?'. The Greek kid's pockets were packed with Drachmas. 'I wonder what percentage 'Evans' was on?'

Shocked, beaten, humiliated, and poorly fed we walked, still full of hope, for defeat and victory must be treated as equal imposters when you're on the pull. To the strip. As we turned the corner there it was our Mecca, our Nirvana, our Destiny, our, our shithole.

Our 'strip' was just a street that had been purposely built for holidaymakers. Devoid of all character or feeling. New concrete buildings with huge neon signs on top of them, flashing away to entice you in. 'Is that all it takes?'. But what made it worse were the people, the kids, yobs. Brits abroad. Gangs of young men all dressed up in their football shirts singing their team's anthems. Because they were on holiday, they all wore their team's away shirt as though this was clever. Girls lagging drunk shouting abuse at the boys, and them shouting back. I suppose they were happy and I'm just being a snob, it just wasn't for us or Warren, who was trying to put a brave face on it all.

We tried to make the best of it that night, but by the end of the evening I said, "I'm not staying here. You lads can do what you want but I'm going". Stan, who is an optimist, said tomorrow we could hire a car and go to the place where the girls at the airport had talked about – Lindos. This was agreed on and the next day I went to hire the car.

When I turned up at the only car hire place in town, a Greek man about fifty said, "No car for the English, English shit, English always damage the car, I don't hire the car". All my persuasion was useless, he was adamant. I'm now thinking that I was totally trapped in this shithole. When I went back to tell the others they roared with laughter at the desperation of this whole mess.

We persuaded Roger, being the oldest and looking the most respectable, to try again with the car hire and we followed him and watched from a café up the road as he haggled with the Greek man. We could see that he was initially getting the same response but eventually convinced him that he wasn't going to damage his car, and came away with our escape.

Pulling up at Lindos that evening was like entering an oasis. Immediately we knew this was for us. No cars can enter the town, just donkeys, on account of the narrow-cobbled walkways. Rooftop restaurants all busy but with a quietness about the place. That Greek feeling, that if you are captivated by, you yearn for in the winter months.

We spent the most part of our holiday in Lindos, driving up every night. But we decided that on our last night we should see some other part of the island and Rhodes Town was suggested for our last evening. I had shagged the girl from the airport, so I guess it was time to move on.

We had an alright-ish evening in Rhodes Town, nothing too memorable. Roger had decided to stay in, so it was just the four of us. Walking back to the car to go home a girl, a Scandinavian girl, Swedish I think, ran in front of us screaming her dress all torn. It looked like she was being raped. Running after her were three Greek lads ordering her back. Stan immediately grabbed hold of her to help her, but the blokes were insisting that she go with them.

The girl was pissed as a newt and terrified of these blokes. They were obviously gang-banging her and wanted more. She's now clinging hold of Stan and begging him not to let them take her. Stan's telling these lads to go, and they're shouting back at him to fuck off.

The whole situation is now completely out of control. When things like this happen, I seem to go into an automatic coolness. Whether at sea in a storm, an emergency at work, or trouble in a bar, I just deal with it, no panic. There was now two choices, walk away from the girl, which wasn't an option, or fight. Straight away I summed up the situation. Stan, Warren, and Laurence haven't got a fight in them. I love them all but if your back is against the wall, and now it was, they're useless.

There were three Greek lads, one of them, their obvious leader was massive. I'm not saying that for poetic licence, but he was fucking massive. He looked like Mongo from 'Blazing Saddles'. The other two were just normal blokes; I thought the other three could handle them.

So I just hit him, when I was younger man I used to box, I know how to hit people and he went down. The shock of seeing Mongo sprawled on the floor silenced everyone. The girl ran off, and Mongo's pals bent down to help him, and I said to the others let's just fuck off.

We were walking briskly up the road when I hear, "English, you and me English". Mongo is following me up the road and wants to carry on rucking. I thought 'Fuck, this is one brave bastard'. When you're in the ring and you knock someone down there are two types of fighters that come back at you: stupid ones who just do it automatically because it's expected of them, and angry ones who now want to kill you for embarrassing them. Mongo was angry – really fucking angry.

So, I turned round and beat him up again. This time I wanted to make sure it was finished so I punched the fuck out of him. So much so that my hands were sore. I got up and almost ran to the car; I just wanted to get out of there. As we get to the car which is parked outside a bar I hear him again, "English, you and me English". I am now starting to get frightened. I'm beating him up but he's winning. Then he hit me and it hurt, it really hurt, there's just this pain running through my face and head. We're now fighting again but my hands and face are sore, I've got to find a way to stop him, so I get him by the hair and start smashing his face against the window wipers, where they come out at the bottom of the windscreen. I can hear his teeth breaking on the bottom wipers.

I can hear people shouting, "Break it up", and others shouting "No, let them fight" and I'm thinking, 'Break it up'. Somehow, we come apart and this mad fucker is literally spitting teeth out like something in a film and wants to carry on fighting. I'm standing there thinking, 'How am I going to stop him?' When this big, muscled bloke grabs hold of me and I think, 'Fuck. I can't fight this bloke and Mongo, they'll kill me'. Then the muscled bloke tells me to go, to get out of here, afterwards we realised he was the doorman of the bar. But the way he talked to me, as though he knew something, I just agreed. Then we did the most stupid thing ever. The four of us got in the car.

As soon as we got in the car Mongo, and every other Greek kid outside the bar, start throwing bottles at the car. There's just this sound of smashing glass, bottles, and the car windows. People are kicking the car and there are bottles and fists are coming through the windows. We are all getting punched to fuck and I'm screaming to Warren to drive. He keeps stalling the car and I'm just shouting, "Drive, Warren drive". He was getting punched in the face and I knew that if he started fighting back we were in real, real serious danger.

Anyway, we finally get away but we've driven down a dead-end road. We have to drive back past the bar. All the Greek kids knew this and were waiting for us to come back. Warren can't just drive through a load of people, so he stops and the whole punching and bottle throwing starts again. Warren does the most stupid thing ever and starts bibbing his horn at the blokes to get out the way. Afterwards we couldn't stop laughing at that, Warren politely bibbing whilst they're trying to maim us.

Eventually we get away. The relief of driving down the road and my adrenaline pumping makes me get a fit of giggles. All a sudden the four of us are pissing ourselves laughing. I turn around to Stan, and he says I need to go to hospital. I just shrug this off and say, "I'll be alright". When we get back in the apartment, I look in the mirror and say to Stan, "I need to go to hospital". My eye is swelling up as I look at it, and the skin is splitting open as the swelling increases.

Stan took me to a hospital, all the way back to Rhodes Town. We go in and there's a Greek doctor in a white coat smoking as he prods my eye. He just sees me as another British hooligan in his home, so he doesn't give a fuck about me or my eye. He rubbed it really hard to see if there was any glass in it, that hurt, it hurt as much as when Mongo hit it.

I want to tell him that I'm not a hooligan that all this happened because we stopped a girl being raped. But I know it's pointless. So he stitched my eye up without numbing it, still smoking. That was the pits.

I'm also laying there and I'm thinking, 'If Mongo had had a knife, I might be getting stitched up like that in my stomach'. I got really frightened and started shaking. Shock and all that I suppose.

All of a sudden, the police come in and start asking questions. Stan explains everything. Because he was older and obviously not a Brit abroad looking for trouble, the police believed him and went away. The doctor, now warmed to me, offered me a fag. I was glad that happened. He also told me there was a man next door having extensive surgery on his face and teeth because they were in such a mess. At the time this pleased me, in fact I wanted to punch the air and shout, "YES."

What happened next will stay with me for the rest of my life. Stan takes me back and we walk down for a coffee and a fag; sleep wasn't an option. We're outside the café and we see Roger drive the car back to the hire place. The owner comes out with his clip board to check for minor damage and looks at the car. You have to imagine this, every pane of glass is smashed out, every panel is kicked in, and every light is smashed. The roof is bent in; there's blood all over the bonnet. The car is full of glass. This car is as fucked as it can be, and Roger is trying to explain about the girl and all that. This man is in shock. He's looking at the car, and then at Roger, jumping up and down. He's trying to talk but can't get any words out. He's having a fit.

Stan and I are in raptures. I'm laughing so much I can't breathe. Every time I laugh my eye hurts, but I can't stop laughing. I honestly thought I was going to die from laughing. Everyone has had those belly laughs; they're not that common and you remember them. This was my biggest. I know that part of it was the release of stress. But even if I hadn't of been in a fight, seeing that man's face was and always will be the funniest moment of my life.

Foot note

I wrote this in my thirties. Reading over it now I realise how full of myself I was then, but I was. Confident to the extreme. As Mickey Dripping always said about me, "If I was a box of chocolates, I'd eat myself". That man in this story is now in his sixties, long gone. I heard a poem that's very poignant.

You didn't know me then

I haven't always been this old

I haven't always felt this cold

A time was I was young and bold

You didn't know me then

I didn't always look this way

I didn't used to sleep all day

I used to dance the night away

You didn't know me then

You never knew the troubadour

Who fell in love with the girl next door

And sung for her Chanson D'Amour

You didn't know me then

You never knew the Warrior the Lover or the Friend

You never knew my glory days

You didn't know me then

Don't judge me now on what you see and don't judge on what you think is me

I was you before you was me

You didn't know me then

It's true my youth has left me

But I'm sure you will allow

If you didn't know me then

Then you don't know me now

- Chris Ross

Bits of Prose

These are writings that I have tried to live my life by. I've failed many times, but I have tried.

There's this fella, he's an executive of a finance company in the City of London. He's trying to get the kids ready for their private school. He's got to drop them off because his wife has a yoga class. He's got a meeting on the golf course at ten. His emails keep pinging; his home phone and his mobile phone keep ringing. And he's trying to digest the news from *The Financial Times*.

All of a sudden there's a knock on the door. He begrudgingly opens the door. There's a man in a long black coat with his hood up, you can hardly see his face and he's carrying a scythe. The fella says, "What do you want mate?" and the man says, "I'm Mister Death, come with me". The fella says, "Oh look mate I haven't got time for this" and goes to shut the door. Mister Death puts his foot in the door and says, "You're dead, you must come with me". The fella says, "I don't understand" and Mister Death explains, "You had a heart attack ten minutes ago, it's over, and you must come with me".

The fella is in shock, he's trying to process the information that his life is over, and all the while

Mister Death is harrying him to hurry up. He asks, "What do I do? What should I bring?" Mister Death says, "Well it can be lonely where you're going; you might want to bring some things with you".

So, the fella thinks 'I know I'll bring my house'. So, he says to his house "Come on House we're going to the other side". House says, "I'm not going anywhere; my foundations are set in this beautiful Surrey countryside. You've just finished that big extension on the side. You've built that gorgeous swimming pool in the grounds. I'm a listed building, I have status here, where you're going, I'll have no worth, I lose my status". The fella says, "But I've spent fortunes on you". House says, "Someone else will buy me straight away and they will take care of me, I'm staying here".

Mister Death says "Hurry up"

So, the fella thinks, 'I know my car'. He goes into the garage and says "Car, come on, we're going to the other side". Car says, "I'm not going anywhere, I'm a classic E-type Jag, I have kudos here, I'm worshiped". The fella says, "But I've spent fortunes on you, I've adored you, I've polished you every Sunday". Car says, "Someone else will buy me straight away and they will treat me exactly the same, that won't happen where you're going".

Mister Death says, "Hurry up; I've got another three to do this morning".

The fella thinks 'Money. I'll bring my money'. He goes into the front room to find his money. He sees a big pound note sitting in his favourite chair, he's wearing sunglasses. He has a blonde girl either side of him giggling, cozying up to him, and he's smoking a big cigar. He says, "Money come on we're going to the other side". Money takes a big, long drag on his cigar and blows it in the fella's face. After a long pause Money says, "Go with you to the other side! Don't be stupid, I have no worth where you're going, no respect, no one adores me over there. We like it here girls, don't we?" and the two blondes push their breasts in and giggle even more.

Mister Death says, "You really must hurry up". The fella says, "Well who else should I ask?". Mister Death says, "Have you tried knowledge and good deeds?" The fella says, "Who?", "Knowledge and good deeds".

The fella walks into the library and realises he hadn't been in there for years. He sees a man sitting at a desk researching something or another. The fella says, "I recognise you, you look familiar". The man says "I'm your knowledge. You used to spend a lot of time with me at school and when you went to university, but you haven't bothered with me for years". The fella says, "Will you come with me to the other side?" The man says "Yes, I will come with you, but I don't know what good I will be to you. We're strangers now". He finally asks, "Do you know where my good deeds are?" And the man says, "Yes, he's down in the basement".

The fella goes down to the basement; he can hear movement right at the back of the basement, in a place he has never been before. There's hardly any light and he sees this decrepit, weak, wheezing old man. The fella says, "Who are you?" and the man says, "I'm your good deeds". The fella says, "You look awful". The man explains, "I'm sorry, but you never spend any time on me, you have always neglected me, and I have become weak in the process". The fella asks, "Will you come with me too the other side?" and Good Deeds says, "Yes, I will go with you, but I don't know I'll be any good too you".

Anyway, the fella, Knowledge and Good Deeds go with Mister Death to the other side.

Desiderata

Go placidly amid the noise and the haste, and remember what peace there may be in silence.
As far as possible, without surrender, be on good terms with all persons.

Speak your truth quietly and clearly; and listen to others, even to the dull and the ignorant; they too have their story.

Avoid loud and aggressive persons; they are vexatious to the spirit. If you compare yourself with others, you may become vain or bitter, for always there will be greater and lesser persons than yourself.

Enjoy your achievements as well as your plans. Keep interested in your own career, however humble; it is a real possession in the changing fortunes of time.

Exercise caution in your business affairs, for the world is full of trickery. But let this not blind you to what virtue there is; many persons strive for high ideals, and everywhere life is full of heroism.

Be yourself. Especially do not feign affection. Neither be cynical about love; for in the face of all aridity and disenchantment, it is as perennial as the grass.

Take kindly the counsel of the years, gracefully surrendering the things of youth.

Nurture strength of spirit to shield you in sudden misfortune. But do not distress yourself with dark imaginings. Many fears are born of fatigue and loneliness.

Beyond a wholesome discipline, be gentle with yourself. You are a child of the universe no less than the trees and the stars; you have a right to be here.

And whether or not it is clear to you, no doubt the universe is unfolding as it should. Therefore, be at peace with God, whatever you conceive Him to be. And whatever your labours and aspirations, in the noisy confusion of life, keep peace in your soul. With all its sham, drudgery and broken dreams, it is still a beautiful world. Be cheerful. Strive to be happy.

- Max Ehrmann

If

If you can keep your head when all about you
Are losing theirs and blaming it on you,

If you can trust yourself when all men doubt you,

But make allowance for their doubting too;

If you can wait and not be tired by waiting,

Or being lied about, don't deal in lies,

Or being hated, don't give way to hating,

And yet don't look too good, nor talk too wise:

If you can dream—and not make dreams your master;

If you can think—and not make thoughts your aim;

If you can meet with Triumph and Disaster

And treat those two impostors just the same;

If you can bear to hear the truth you've spoken

Twisted by knaves to make a trap for fools,

Or watch the things you gave your life to, broken,

And stoop and build 'em up with worn-out tools:

If you can make one heap of all your winnings

And risk it on one turn of pitch-and-toss,

And lose, and start again at your beginnings

And never breathe a word about your loss;

If you can force your heart and nerve and sinew

To serve your turn long after they are gone,

And so hold on when there is nothing in you

Except the Will which says to them: 'Hold on!'

If you can talk with crowds and keep your virtue,

Or walk with Kings—nor lose the common touch,

If neither foes nor loving friends can hurt you,

If all men count with you, but none too much;

If you can fill the unforgiving minute

With sixty seconds' worth of distance run,

Yours is the Earth and everything that's in it,

And—which is more—you'll be a Man, my son!
- Rudyard Kipling

~ Definition of War...Two working class blokes at either end of a rifle. ~

Marvin Hagler

My part in helping him win the world title

1980 Alan Minter is the World Middle Weight Champion. He is defending his title against Marvin Hagler and was favourite to win. I was Minter's biggest fan. He was the president of our boxing club, and we had our Christmas do there every year. I would also go to watch him train at the Thomas Beckett pub on the Old Kent Road. I loved him, we had a proper World Champion.

Fight night. I'm ten rows from the ring, an aisle seat and I've got a sweat top on that says 'Alan Minter'. Where I was sitting was exactly where Marvin Hagler was walking down to the ring. The fight was at Wembley Arena and was full of yobs, not true fight fans, just hooligans all shouting out racist stuff it was horrible. As Hagler is about to walk by there is this tosser screaming out "You fucking n***** you black c***". I could go on but you get the picture, it was awful.

I don't know if you've ever seen Hagler walk into the ring, he wore a blue robe with his hood up and his face covered in Vaseline. He was a mean looking bastard. He can hear this tosser shouting out this crap and stops and turns around. The tosser has sat down and hid behind his seat and Hagler is staring at me and I shit myself. He looks at me for what seemed an eternity but was probably a few seconds and his eyes say, "If I didn't have something better to do like win the world title, I'd smash the fuck out of you." I freeze, couldn't talk. I wanted to say, "I'm sorry, it wasn't me, I want Minter to win but not like this." Luckily, he turns back and walks to the ring.

The Best of Times

What happened next was incredible; Hagler just beats Minter up in three rounds, easily. Any fight fan knew we had seen the start of something really, really special.

The Worst of Times

Then all these so-called 'fight fans', actually scum started throwing bottles in the ring, these were coming down from right up in the stands and were so dangerous. Hagler never had his belt placed on him, which is what he deserved. He had to be escorted from the ring by the police. I remember seeing Harry Carpenter and Henry Cooper holding chairs above their heads to protect themselves. I felt ashamed of my country, ashamed of the way Hagler was treated, and ashamed of this scum.

But as I say I like to think that his anger at me as he went into the ring helped him win the world title.

~ Time flies, Bruce Forsyth has been dead for seven years now. Not many people know this, but he died from a nasty seizure. NASTY SEIZURE to see you NASTY. ~

Benidorm

Three of us outside a café, in Benidorm. In the eighties it was the place to be for clubs and girls. It was a mad place then but now they've cleaned it up and send old people there on their holidays. I went out with a girl once whose mother used to holiday there in the fifties. She had this big picture of the bay with only one or two classy hotels strategically placed along the shore. It was the most beautiful picture of a Spanish coastline I had ever seen. Boy did we all fuck that place up.

Anyway, we're outside this café, Mark, Jimmy and me, and three Spanish girls come off the beach and sit down in the café. They were stunning, I mean really stunning. Young tanned and Spanish. One of them, Chus, had those Spanish eyes. In the seventies working class homes always had two mementoes of their Iberian travels. One was a little black fighting bull that sat on the telly. The other was a picture of a Spanish girl with naked shoulders, long dark hair and these massive dark eyes. Great big dark brown eyes, almost like a Jersey cow.

I'm sitting there drowning in this girl's eyes. I've fallen in and I'm drowning. I'm sat next to the girl who was obviously the model for the painting that replaced the three china ducks. I'm staring at her and she's giggling at me, in fact the three of them are taking the piss out of me. But they don't speak a word of English, so I don't know what they are saying. I asked the owner of the café, an English woman, (she became our go between, translator, a kind of patriarch for us) to ask them to come over. They did and through this café owner we all got to know each other and arranged a date for that night all six of us. Our patriarch loved it.

The other two girls were called Abar and Monse. They kind of hitched up with Mark and Jimmy but nothing too serious. I on the other hand had fallen madly in love with Chus. Her skin dark and tanned and young and lovely; her hair, long, straight, black. And all the time these gorgeous black eyes. Staring, staring.

We spent four days with them. That was a really good time. Neither Chus nor I could speak a word of the others' language, it was all signs, signals, innuendo, laughter, touch. I loved it. I really loved it.

When you're on your holidays there's always a song that brings you straight back to that time, you know this, it even has a name, and it's called 'our song'. Our song was 'Waiting for A Train'. It was big in all the clubs at the time. It was kind of a rap but had a catchy hook on the keyboard. There's a line in it that I always thought was funny 'I wonder what's cooking at the house tonight, stew and beans'. It meant fuck all but I just liked it. I used to hold Chus by the shoulders, look straight into her eyes and in my best passionate voice sing it to her. She loved it. When we were in a club and it came on, she would wait for me to sing it to her. What was mad was it wasn't even a sexy line, but it made me laugh in a cute way.

Everything was bang on, everything but the sex. She was a good Catholic girl. I was a Catholic boy but that never seemed to stop me. It was a "No" at the end of the evening and off home. How come the only English word she knew was 'No'.

Then we went out on our last night. It was different; we both knew that our holiday thing had come to an end. We said that we would write but we both knew it was over and it was sad. The other thing that was different was her; she was cooler, more composed. I didn't know it then, but she had made up her mind that she was going to fuck me that night and had that air of a woman totally in control. Men are fucked when women behave like this, or men like me are. We lose all power, all reason. Never understood why women don't rule the world.

So, after another night of clubs and bars, I start to walk her home, but she leads me out along the beach. Everyone knows this feeling. The sky is black but full of stars, the air is warm, save a sea breeze and you can hear the waves crashing on the shore. She's sitting on the sand and has kicked her sandals off. I'm sitting next to her, and I can smell her skin. I'm kissing her shoulders and I'm fucking tingling with excitement. My bollocks are about to explode from her sending me home every night. Then she looks at me with those eyes and says the only other line of English I ever heard her say, "No, baby."

She lays back and I gorge myself on her body. The detail is irrelevant and disrespectful to her to repeat it. But I will tell you about the end, which is the whole point of this story.

We're both about to come and she grabs my hair and is pulling like she wants to rip it out of my head. I'm so turned I don't give a fuck, and she starts really panting heavy, stroke, breathing, stoke, screaming. And when she orgasms, she shouts out, "Stew and beans". My fucking head is spinning. Part of me wants to laugh, part of me wants to yell with pain with all the hair pulling and I just want to come but remember the 'No, baby' and roll over. Fucked.

I lay back and I am thinking about what she said – "Stew and beans". In her head this was obviously a sexy thing to say, it was just so funny hearing her say it. I then think about her next romance with an English bloke, who, when he makes love to her and she screams out "Stew and beans" will wonder what on earth is going on. The thought of this makes me roar with laughter. But I can't explain any of this to her. Chus, thinking I'm laughing at her, storms off with the hump and I follow trying to placate her.

~ I've been reading a book on how to please a woman with foreplay. But the first few chapters were boring, so I skipped past them. ~

Beautiful Asian Eyes

It's the mid-eighties at work; I'm riding the emergency tender appliance at Euston Fire Station. This fire engine carried all the special cutting equipment for car accidents or people under trains etc. About teatime we get called to a child with his hand stuck in machinery. When we get there, it was a cottage industry sausage making factory at the back of this Asian family's house. The child's job was to push the sausage meat into the mincer, where sausages come out the end. He, being too young, had pushed his hand in too far and the mincer had pulled his arm down as far as it can go, and his fingers are coming out of the end with all the rest of the sausage meat. What added to the problem was a couple of fingers are still moving so all the nerve endings hadn't been severed. The medics asked if it was possible to cut his arm out without severing the nerve endings so he might still have some use of his hand.

After some consultation with the officer in charge, I grabbed the cengar saw, this was a saw that was powered by gas bottles and so had more power. It was a great tool at the time but now most builders would have better cutting tools. Using acetylene gas cutting was not an option for obvious reasons.

I managed to get the casing off quite easily and could see his arm stretched and moving down the machine. The main mechanism of the machine was an Archimedes screw running down the middle which moved the sausage meat along. (Archimedes was an Ancient Greek inventor; his 'screw' could lift water vertically). The problem was I couldn't cut the screw in half; I just seemed to be cutting and following the curvature of the screw.

I wasn't making any progress. The medics are getting anxious, they want this kid on his way to hospital, my officer can sense the delay and is getting frustrated, but I just can't cut this fucking thing in half. The child has obviously been sedated to the hilt, but he just keeps staring at me with these beautiful Asian eyes. Looking at me for help but I just can't help him. I was getting in a bit of a mess with the stress of it, but somehow after more cutting we got most of his arm and hand out.

Go back to the station. Whenever children die or are hurt a real sense of depression descends on the station, as well as anger at the parents or some other driver or something. It goes in the end, but you can sense it. There's sadness on the station. Anyway, we sit down to our dinner, it was 'sausage and mash' the reason I know this is because halfway through the meal a workmate pulls a bit of gristle out of his mouth and says ""Ere there's gristle in the mash", after inspecting the gristle he realises it's a finger. He stands up in disgust and says, "Some cunt has put that kid's finger in the mash". We fell about laughing, couldn't stop laughing.

Foot note.

The end of this story sounds barbaric, disgusting as though we were animals not firefighters. But this was in the eighties, at that time there was no counselling service in the brigade. We dealt with death, mutilation, appalling things on a regular basis. I'm not whinging or making myself out to be a hero, it's just how it was. You also had to learn how to deal with it as well. One way was dark humour, it works, I don't know why it just does.

> ~ Later on in my life I was diagnosed with Post Traumatic Stress Disorder (PTSD) and retired from the brigade with it. Don't blame any emergency worker from dealing with anything in the best way they know how. ~

Leaving Home

1983 I'm twenty-one years old; I had bought my first house with a girl called Nicky; she was lovely. It was a Victorian terraced house, and I had set about renovating it. When I had done enough work to make the main bedroom liveable I moved in. I couldn't wait to get in my first own home.

The night before I had packed all my stuff and put it in the hallway, all ready to go in the morning. My mum come out, looked at all my belongings and said, "You're all ready then son". Then this sadness descended on us that neither of us was expecting. Her little boy was going, our time, me living there, was over and it hurt. My mum went away, and I know she would have cried. I got in the bath and cried my eyes out. We hid this from each other, and I'll never know why.

In the morning a big breakfast was made. You can't leave home on an empty stomach, packed my stuff and left. I give her a cuddle on the way out, but nothing was said, no big speech from either of us. I remember Laurie Lee spoke about his own identical experience, in 'Cider with Rosie' he said, "I had never felt so fat with time" a beautiful piece of prose. I could not have matched the sentiment but knew the exact same feeling.

Worked all day on the house, so excited sorting stuff out. One of the big days of your life. I didn't stop all day and about six in the evening I was starving but cooking or a takeaway wasn't wanted so I rang up my mum and asked her if I could come and get some tea. She said, "Of course you can son" and I was back in a jiffy, back in my old seat being fed. I left home for eight hours!

Years later when Dan left to come and live with me and start a job, Dee had come to settle him into my house. Dee cried all the way home because she said that it was over, their time living together as twins, that Dan had left home. I tried to console her that nothing was over, that they would just sleep in different buildings now. Dan went home for the weekend two weeks later.

~ I was drunk last night Mother, I was drunk the night before, but if you forgive me Mother, I won't get drunk anymore.

I was courting last night Mother, I was courting the night before, but if you forgive me Mother, I won't go courting no more.

Cause I'm skint tonight, Mother, like I was skint the night before, but if you lend me ten bob Mother, I won't be skint anymore.

So let's dance tonight Mother, let's dance like the night before, let's dance and sing Mother and keep troubles away from the door.

So I'll hold you tonight, Mother, like I held you the night before, cause the saddest day of my life Mother, is when I can't hold you no more. ~

Letters of Thanks

For a number of years, I was involved with the Fire Brigades Union (F.B.U) this was amongst my happiest times in the fire brigade. I became an official, and represented firefighters at discipline cases, medical appeals, and grievances. I often feel I did my best work as a Union Official and met some of the best people in the fire brigade. It was my most enjoyable time. Here are a couple of letters of thanks I received.

Dear Brendan

It's been quite some time since I last spoke to you, just over a year now. I say it now "Thank you for representing me that day at the hearing, I am grateful".

Over the past year or so I have turned over the events of that day and the previous two to three years over in my mind, all the indicators, points and little twists that occurred between me and the other parties. The first incidents through to taking matters into my own hands and the consequences of my actions. It won't happen again.

After the day of the incident, I was transferred to Euston fire station. Things started to fall apart at the seams. I didn't know anyone to confide in at Euston or express my worst fears. Losing my job was at the top of my list and the stigma that carries. I withdrew into myself, kept quiet and treated everyone the same, even yourself. Don't get me wrong, I told everyone what happened from the word go.

That first meeting at the F.B.U. offices I felt uneasy, told you everything that had happened and left. I didn't feel too confident in you. Hue Elvin who knows you tried to reassure me, even though he could see that I had my doubts about the case, you and myself. For the first time ever, I felt at a loss.

As the Hearing drew closer you came to Euston to go over the questions you would put to me. Before we went upstairs you asked the blue watch if we could have stand easy with them and they agreed. The questions and answers session went well; any faults were ironed out and then we went downstairs for stand easy. I sat on the opposite side of the table from you. I remember you telling me that you had served on this station, knowing that this is the most militant watch on the station, full of strong personalities, whose word, as far as they're concerned, was rule. I sat there silent, quietly watching, I knew what was coming.

When they went for you none of them intended to lose face, but you out manoeuvred them, blunted their attacks, cut away everything until it was laid bare. Spoke to them directly and won them over to your way of thinking by the truth of your words. I sat there and watched and when you had finished, I knew that by the way you carried yourself in those twenty minutes that come the day of the hearing, win or lose, no one else could represent me better than you. I left the station in a better frame of mind.

At the hearing I met Garda (Razuski) for the first time, she's a nice person. It was good to have a friendly face in my corner as well as you, and she put me at ease at once.

Your opening address was brilliant; I sat there amazed during the hearing. What you said on my behalf could not be bettered. All the way through you cut away at everything the prosecution put forward against me and laid it bare for what it was.

When I went into the hearing, I was looking at losing my job and career. When I left at the end with a caution I could not have wished for better. This is only due to the patience, hard work and clever thinking by you, on my behalf.

In the pub afterwards you asked me to write to everyone who gave evidence on my behalf, this I have done. Some didn't believe I could write letters like I did but just like you said, "Say it from the heart" and it works every time.

Maurice Allen

Blue watch, A 23, Euston.

Dear Brendan

I am writing to thank you for your efforts in my recent discipline case. I now realise you went out on a bit of a limb to represent me. For that I am grateful. It is certain that without your support as a representative of the union, the brigade would have felt at liberty to impose an even greater penalty.

I also thank you for understanding my need to ask advice about your abilities. Having seen you at work I will not hesitate to recommend you to anyone who needs help.

I am also very grateful for your personal investment in securing a fair hearing for me. It was clear that you put a lot of time and effort into the preparation of the case. I hope to be able to repay you one day.

John Turner.

~ We live in a democracy, we have no choice about this, that in itself is undemocratic. ~

Throw Her on the Couch

As mentioned before, about 2008 I was diagnosed with Post Traumatic Stress Disorder. I was required by the fire brigade to attended counselling sessions once a month with a brigade councillor. He was a young man and I liked him, I don't know if it was helpful, but it wasn't unpleasant. Sometimes we even got a laugh. I told him once that I knew I was drinking too much but it helped me sleep. At the end of the session, he asked me what I was going to do about all the alcohol, and I said, "Drink it" he had to contain himself from laughing.

I turned up for one session and was introduced to this gorgeous woman in her late twenties. She was dressed in business attire, a white blouse, dark skirt, dark tights and black high heel shoes. She was blonde and wore dark glasses. She looked very professional and business like, but she was beautiful. This look is also a lot of men's sexual fantasia. Anyway, we were introduced and I was asked if I would mind her shadowing my case as she was learning to become a councillor. I had no objection to this. She sat in the corner of the room crossed legged and I had to try to stop myself from staring at her.

At this time, I was placed on medication, if your head is fucked no one really knows what to do with you, so they try all different things. Cognitive Behavioural Therapy, counselling, or medication to see if any of these things help. I was given these tablets to try.

At that time, I was living with a girl called Kate and I just found it hard to come, ejaculate. I thought it was just how I was feeling but after a while I couldn't come at all. Then, a little while later, I couldn't get an erection no matter what I did, I was really worried now. I got hold of the pills and it said on the label at the back these pills might cause erectile dysfunction. I tipped them down the toilet straight away, I wasn't having that.

So, at the counselling session the doctor asked me how I was getting on with the medication. Don't forget I'm in quite a small room there's a couch behind me and this girl is sitting in the corner with her legs crossed and looks stunning. I felt a bit embarrassed talking about this in front of this girl, but the doctor kept insisting how I was getting on. So, I just said, "Doc, I couldn't get it up on them so I threw them away". He then asked if I was alright now, I said, "Fine". But he kept on insisting; he comes over to me, took me by the hand and asked again, was I ok now? I didn't know what he was after, but he asked me again, was I ok now?

I had to stop myself from saying, "Throw her up on the couch and I'll show you".

~ And God said there would be good and obedient women found in all corners of the world. And then he made the world round and laughed his head off. ~

The Snip

I've got three children, Chloe, 32 and Dan and Dee, twins, 21. Dee is short for Cordelia. Chloe being my first was just this all-consuming love. I had never felt love like her before. She meant everything to me. But when the twins come along, and I loved them just as much, what I noticed was that now I had Dan and Dee it sort of thinned my love for Chloe. She was no longer my only child; I had two others who I loved the same. I'm sure every parent goes through this same thing. Anyway, I knew that I can't afford any more thinning of love, I can't share any more time and I certainly can't afford to pay any more money, so I decided to have the snip. A vasectomy.

Saw the doctor and went for my appointment at the hospital. When I got there, I was welcomed by two nurses, both gorgeous, who booked me in. So, me being me, I started flirting with them. Then I had to get changed and put on this gown. I started to get nervous, anxious, even scared. When I walked into the theatre a male nurse, who was really nice, laid me on the operation table and asked me how I was doing. I said, "If you want to know the truth mate, I'm shitting myself". He said, "Well if someone was going to take a knife to my toggle and two, I'd be scarred as well."

So, there's me, a doctor, a male nurse, and the two girl nurses in the operating theatre. I lay down, and the doctor pulls up my gown above my waist. Because I'm shitting myself my cock has withdrawn through fear, into my body, it's about half an inch long. I can see the two girl nurses drop their eyes to look at it. Don't forget I'd been giving it the 'Big 'un' ten minutes ago and I could have just died with embarrassment. 'Why do they have to see that?'. Then I'm given a local anaesthetic, that's a needle in the bollocks. As the doctor was inserting the needle the male nurse held my hand, I thought that was a nice touch. Then, until the anaesthetic takes hold, I'm left on the operating table, lying on my back with my tiny little cock out for everyone to look at.

After a few minutes the doctor comes back and runs a knife down my scrotum, 'my balls', and cuts them open. There was no pain. But run your fingernail down the palm of your hand, there's no pain but you can feel what's happening. I can feel my bollocks being cut open. I was so frightened. He then pulls out whatever you call them tubes from my balls and lances them with some hot tool. Pulling the tubes made me gag and then the smell of my bollocks burning was awful, I thought I was going to be sick. The whole thing was horrendous. And the whole time the male nurse is holding my hand and I'm squeezing his. Finally, I'm stitched up and again no pain, but I can feel the sensation of the needle stitching up my bollocks. Fucking hell, it was fucking awful.

On leaving the doctor says there will be pain afterwards so wear loose fitting pants and trousers, and you will also suffer from bruising. That was an understatement. My bollocks, my cock and that whole area turned to whatever the colour is between black and dark purple, and was really sensitive for weeks.

Finally, I healed and the scariest part of this whole story now starts. I had to test it all out. I had to have a wank. I was frightened that it might feel different, that things have changed. I remember a cat had it done down our street as a kid and the cat lost interest after that. (That's a joke). So, I tentatively do the business and it's all ok. There was no difference in feeling whatsoever. The only difference is the end result. What I was left with was an insipid grey fluid. I remember thinking, 'That wouldn't get anybody pregnant'. This was the whole point, I guess.

~ An unexamined life is not worth living. Socrates. ~

How My Kids Got Their Names

Early nineties, I signed up for an English Literature course, it was at a local comprehensive school, two hours every Wednesday night. It was just 'education for education's sake'. I learnt how to read on this course, how to understand text, find the meaning the author is trying to convey. It was really interesting and better than just talking bollocks in the pub after work.

One of the books we had to study was Shakespeare's King Lear. I learnt so much about him, it's not what I would read by choice but everything you have heard about him is true and more.

Anyway, the story goes like this, my words not his. Lear is a pompous, full of himself, vain fool. He's also a King. He has three daughters Goneril, Regan and Cordelia. He asks his first daughter, "Goneril, tell me how great I am" and Goneril responds, "Father you are the wisest of men, an intellect, full of wisdom and grace". Lear says, "Thank you my daughter, you are also very wise" and bequests her all his northern territory. Her husband smiles at her, well done.

Next, he says, "Regan speak" she says, "Father you are truly the wisest man in the land, I endorse all that

Goneril says and more, I worship you, even with my square inch of pleasure". This is taken as her vagina. Lear says, "Thank you my daughter, I bequest you all my southern lands". Her husband smiles in acceptance.

Lastly, he says, "Cordelia speak" Cordelia says, "I've nothing to say father" and Lear says, "Think again Cordelia, nothing becomes of nothing". She says, "I love you dad, I always have, but I'm not going to gush praise on you to flatter your ego, and I certainly won't love you with my square inch of pleasure, which will be kept for the man I love". Lear, his vanity getting to him, banishes Cordelia from his lands.

Anyway, time goes on and the two daughters connive, squabble, lie, and cheat, and eventually, with the help of their husbands, get all of Lear's lands, all his titles, his money, and banish him from the land.

He's now destitute and walking around Normandy with nothing. In desperation he has knocked on Cordelia's door and asks if he can come in. He knows he has no right to ask for forgiveness. But Cordelia brings him in, welcomes him, gives him a big hug and says, "Dad, I told you then I love you, I still love you now" and forgives him in his hour of need.

On hearing this tale and the way my life seems to pan out I remember thinking, "I need a daughter like Cordelia". So, Dee got her name.

Two heroes of mine are Che Guevara and Chay Bligh. Che Guevara was with Fidel Castro when they landed in Cuba and took over the country. Chay Bligh was the first person to sail single handed around the world the wrong way, against wind currents. I wanted to bastardise these two names and make the name Chey, for my son. Sarah, my wife at the time, wanted to call her son Daniel. So, I said, "Let's wait 'til he comes out, you have to be a bit of a mush to carry the name Chey, let's see what he looks like", Sarah agreed.

When he was born, he was the softest, sweetest looking cherub I had ever seen. Sarah said, "Is he a Chey or a Daniel?" I said, "He's a Daniel". Sarah was pleased. Mind you, there is a football player in the premiership who is called Che Adams, when being interviewed once the interviewer said, "So Che, apart from having the coolest name in the premiership…"

I wasn't involved in choosing my daughter's name, Chloe; no one was bothered about my opinion. Nor was my surname put on her birth certificate. When it came to money and paying though, I was always given priority.

However, I do like the name Chloe French, especially if you put the accent over the é so it looks French. Chloé is, after all, a French luxury fashion house.

~ If politics changed anything they would ban it. ~

A Narcissist

A Narcissistic Personality Disorder (NPD) is a mental health condition in which people have an unreasonably high sense of their own importance. They need, want, and seek people to admire them. People with this disorder lack the ability to care or understand the feelings of others. They do not understand the effect their behaviour has on other people.

One possible cause of NPD is, in parent-child relationships, too much adoration is given, that doesn't match the child's achievements. Parents believing their child to be, or treating them, more special than they actually are.

As the child grows, an NPD Parent will be over possessive and controlling, seeing the child as an extension of themselves. They lack the ability to love fully and unconditionally.

My father Brendan French was brought up in Dublin by my grandparents Willy and Annie French. The family grew in between the war years when work, good food, and money were scarce. They were a Catholic family, so six children. Four years before my father was born, another brother, Richie had died. He was coughing up blood as a child. I don't know the exact cause of his death, but lack of money in the house is a good guess. This obviously devastated my grandparents. Then my father and his twin Gerard were born. Gerard died within a year, again the root source being the lack of money that brings malnutrition.

My grandfather was not lazy or a bad provider. He was a good dad; the hard times and poverty is to blame.

Again, my grandparents were devastated and felt guilt over this second child loss and overcompensated by gushingly loving and praising my father. All my uncles and aunties said he was always the favourite, he was treated special.

I do not blame my grandparents for the way they behaved. I have twins, if one of them had died as a child I firmly believe Sarah and I would have overcompensated with love on the other twin, to the detriment of their upbringing.

As with my father, a classic environment was created for a narcissist to be nurtured and brought up. My father had NPD.

How did this manifest as I was growing up.

My father hardly ever worked. This was not because of the lack of work, this is because he believed he was too good to work, that work was for other people.

If he ever did work, and he was a good bricklayer, the money he earned should be spent on himself, and not on bills or rent. Obviously, no one can live like this, it's financially impossible. So, my father went on the dole at a very early age, late thirties I think and never came off it. He also married a hard-working Irish woman, my mum, who worked two jobs all her life to pay the bills and bring up me and my sister.

I used to call him the 'Brick a-loo-loo Boy'. He would start on a job on Monday, happy, singing asking for another brick a-loo-loo. Tuesday he would be quiet, everyone asking him why he wasn't singing today. Wednesday he would come to work, cause an argument, ask to be paid up and go on the piss, start drinking. I've had a million builders in Bromley tell me this story.

He would come home drunk, tell my mum he hadn't been paid, a fight would ensue. My mum smashing the fuck out of him, screaming "Where's the fucking money?". They'd make up after three days. He would get another job after a couple of weeks and the same process would repeat itself, over and over again. This was part of my childhood.

As previously stated, a narcissist has to constantly prove how great they are, this can lead to bullying others around them. This led to my father hitting me. At the time it was called a 'good hiding', the child needs to be admonished for his wrongdoing by physical punishment. I now know that what happened to me was child abuse. No other words for it.

My father would be in a bad mood, probably because he had no money for drink. My mum and my sister would be out of the house; I would be playing in the park or at the back of the flats and be called up. I knew I was going to get a 'good hiding'. They were never just administered; first of all, he would tell me what was about to happen to me. This would frighten the shit out of me, which was after all, its purpose. He would then proceed to beat me. I would cover up in a little ball on the floor to protect myself and he would try to find a way in to hurt me. Once this had been accomplished and his ego satisfied, I was allowed to go back outside and play. Again, this was part of my childhood.

This affected me, as I try to analyse my own life, in four ways:

I learnt that fighters fight in patterns. My father would throw two left hands and then a big right hand, every time. Once you learn the pattern you should be able to avoid most punches. This lesson I carried over into amateur boxing.

If you keep kicking a dog in the end it will bite you. All the time this was happening I was growing, getting more mature. By the time I was seventeen and boxing at the time, I had had enough. I was called up, he wanted to start an argument over nothing, and this time I smashed the fuck out of him. I sat across his chest and constantly punched him in the face for ages. If you knew my father his nose was slightly twisted, I did this when I was seventeen. He had to go to hospital. This behaviour is obviously abhorrent. To this day, I wake up in a nightmare punching my father in the face.

It made me loose fear. I was so frightened of him as a child; when he was telling me how he was going to beat me, show me what a man he was, telling me how hard he was. Since that time, nothing has frightened me as much as that.

Further to this he would always let me down, always put himself first at times to my astonishment. By the time I was an adult I had finished with him. I had to just accept it. There's a song by Ian McNab, 'Fire Inside My Soul'. It has a line 'My dad died when I was twenty, I didn't cry but it tore me up inside'. Every time I hear it, I think about him.

The only good to come out of all of this, I have failed as a father time and time again, losing my temper, shouting, missing some show of affection, something of that nature. But I have never hit or got physical with my children, ever. It had to stop with me.

The symptom that all narcissists' children are an extension of themselves was so evident. My father praised me all the time, or the correct adjective would be bragged. He constantly bragged about me, but he never once was talking about me. He was talking about himself, the only reason I achieved anything was because I was his son, he produced me, he was the catalyst, the reason, that made everything happen.

Also, narcissistic fathers court sibling rivalries, they need allies. He certainly wasn't going to get one out of me. I have no relationship with my sister at all; it is broken beyond all repairs. My father courted this, he encouraged it.

Lastly, I have referred to my father as father; I have tried to be objective. In truth I never called him father or dad; you have to earn the title to be called 'Dad'. I called him Pat all my adult life, which is kind of short for Paddy which he hated being called.

I recently heard that when your children call you dad, and they want to come and spend time with you, you have achieved the ultimate that you can achieve in life. I'm not doing too badly.

~ Poor old Gerard, he's got a lot to answer for. Rest in Peace uncle. ~

Amnesty International

One thing I'm proud of is that I was the Amnesty International (A.I.) delegate for the Fire Brigades Union (F.B.U.). I used to be a lot more politically active than I am now, attended conferences etc. I enjoyed that time.

For those that don't know, A.I. was formed in 1961 when an English barrister, Peter Benenson, heard that two students in Portugal had been given seven years imprisonment for toasting freedom in a bar. Its main purpose is to make sure all countries conform to the Universal Declaration of Human Rights. A.I. campaigns on the individual's behalf. Always support A.I. and let freedom reign.

What follows is a report I had written for the F.B.U. It was printed in our magazine:

The delegations as a whole seemed to be made up of, on one hand, what I would call woolly liberals and on the other, trades unionists. But certainly, all good people and I was glad to be there.

You'll be pleased to know that A.I. is subject to all the same internal rule changes and bureaucratic nightmares that we are.

The way the conference was run was to split into workshops, to debate different issues and then come back to the main plenary sessions to vote on the motions. This worked well, with people given time to debate motions thoroughly, and having time to get your head around the arguments before voting.

There were also various speakers. The two who made the biggest impression on me were Fergal Kane, the BBC correspondent who covered the Rwandan war, and a woman who spoke for the Mothers of the Disappeared in Chile. She thanked A.I. for all the work and support the movement had given to the Mothers of the Disappeared, and also thanked Great Britain and the Prime Minister for detaining Pinochet for 513 days. She sees this as some kind of victory that they had to cling to, as there was very little else. The fact is that her son was dragged from his bed by the secret police under the Pinochet regime, probably tortured and then killed, and is still missing after 15 years. And all she had as any kind of solace was that, that bastard Pinochet spent 513 in a safe house in the stockbroker belt of Surrey, made you angry to say the least.

The next speaker Fergal Kane, war correspondent for the BBC, told how he was hailed as a hero for his coverage of the Rwandan War. He of course disputes this. He told a story of how a group of children aged between five and sixteen hid from the soldiers in a convent. The Mother Superior was frightened for her own life, as harbouring children was a crime punishable by death. She of course had no choice. When the soldiers eventually came, the children didn't bother to run or hideaway, they simply knew it was their turn to die. They assembled in the courtyard, and with a look of fear inevitability on their faces, were loaded into the truck, never to be seen again.

When Fergal tried to report this to the world's media, the soldiers came to his bed at night with a rifle pointed at his head, he was told to leave. This now plays heavily on his conscience. Don't judge Fergal too hard; what would you do in his situation.

Anyway, onto the voting. After an executive meeting Geoff and I voted as follows.

1. That all countries sign up to the Internal Labour Organisations recommendations.

2. That the Freedom of Information Act be returned to Parliament and not become statute until it achieves what it was designed to do.

3. That Amnesty International is allowed to speak up against the effect of sanctions in places like Iraq and Cuba. They can't of course condemn sanctions outright as this would seem to be political and Amnesty guards its nonpolitical reputation fiercely.

4. That Amnesty wait until October (when the report from the International Committee is finalised) to launch their campaign against female genitalia mutilation in Africa. The reason we voted this way was to start unprepared could damage Amnesty's worldwide reputation.

5. That Dr Taye Woldesmiate, President of the Ethiopian Teachers Association is recognised as a prisoner of conscience.

6. That there is increased vigilance to protect the Human Rights in Northern Ireland.

7. That the term M.S.P. (Military Security and Police Transfers) be referred to as the arms trade.

8. That Amnesty condemns the Government's treatment of asylum seekers and the hate campaign the British press is now conducting against them.

All the above motions were, I'm pleased to say, carried.

A.I. is like every other movement, short of money and needs your support. But more importantly your voice. It's a simple numbers game, if enough of us shout, they have to listen.

~ Reading back over this now is strange, seems so long ago. ~

The Tree Hugging Course

London Fire Brigade 90's, the powers that be had decided to send all managers across the brigade on a new type of course called 'Value Centred Leadership'. The purpose of the course is that if you are in any position of authority in the brigade, you should place valuing your co-workers at the centre of your leadership. Us firefighters affectionately called it the 'Tree Hugging Course' and were all very cynical of it.

It was one of the best courses I ever attended in the brigade. A great team ran it, and something I particularly liked was you were on the course with a cross section of the brigade. Girls from pay section, the team from ropes and lines, civilian staff from personnel, personnel from equalities, as well as other firefighters in different roles. People who all worked under the umbrella of the London Fire Brigade, but you never personally met.

It lasted about four days, and all sorts of activities were carried out, some really interesting and yes, if you wanted to hug a tree this was encouraged.

One exercise at the end of the last day, was to write your name at the top of a piece of paper and pass it to the person on your right, they would then write comments about you, their view of you after spending time on the course with you. We all did this about each other. What follows is what was written on my page. I've always been really proud of it.

Brendan

You are so honest it puts me to shame.

I like the way you can quote verse and relate it to matter subject.

Your fair and equitable approach.

The best thing I like about Brendan is his honesty.

Articulate, likeable, gusty, confident nice guy.

Pleasure to meet you Brendan, I admire your honesty, and I too think you are a natural leader. All the very best.

A person not afraid to show his opinion whatever it is, very courageous.

A caring person who takes his time to find out about someone then helps them all he can.

An intelligent, kind, tender, powerful and compassionate man.

An honest man who wants to put the world to right and feels he can make a difference and prepared to try.

Courageous and honest person.

Tender, kind and compassionate.

An honest and intelligent guy. Would always do everything he could to make life better for you. Not afraid to voice his views and I admire him for that.

Strong and funny, not scared to give his opinion - good stuff.

Strong and confident character and loving father.

~ My mother made me, and I know I must have Irish blood in me because I wake up with a hangover every day. Noel Gallagher. ~

Heaven and Hell

When I was at Euston Fire Station, Great Ormond Street Children's Hospital was on our ground. We would constantly get called to an AFA (Automatic Fire Alarm) at the hospital. AFA's are the pain in the arse for firefighters; they are very rarely are a fire, but we get called to them all the time. Of course, they must be attended but I would say 90% of the time they are a false alarm.

We would get called to Great Ormond Street all the time, it was a regular part of our working life, but it was always harrowing to go. The reason is the wards are full of very sick children. Kids with shaved heads and tubes in their arms. No one wants to see this. A lot of firemen, and they were all men then, were fathers and this was stressful for them, imagining their own children being there. They would turn up, check wherever the alarm panel was sending them too and walk out quickly looking at the floor. Not making eye contact with anyone. They weren't being cruel or unkind; it was just too painful for them.

For whatever reason I couldn't do that. I have always been able to connect with children, I like children. So, when we had finished checking the alarm sensor, I would see a little kid lying in his bed with the shaved head and tubes in his arm I would stop and ask his name. I tried to make it fun; I'd take my helmet off and put it on his head and tell him when he grows up, he can be a fireman. I'd try and get a smile out of him and give him a laugh for a short time. Normally, especially if it was the evening, their parents would be sitting with them and they were so pleased to see their little girl or boy smiling, it was just a release for them.

The thing is, it was a ward, there were loads of other kids in there and all the parents wanted their child to talk to the fireman, their child to have a quick smile. So, I would have to go around every bed, it took hours. The doctors and nurses loved it as well, they try to make the ward a happy place for the child, but can you imagine how hard this must be for them. Children are dying in there and they have to deal with this all the time.

It would take me ages to get around the ward, Richard Lockwood (a fireman at Euston) said to me once we all knew that if you were on the shout we would be there for hours, waiting for you to talk to the kids.

Great Ormond Street Hospital is in my opinion one of the greatest things about this country. If you want to know what hell looks like, it's a ward full of sick children, with cancer or tuberculosis, with their heads shaved and tubes in their arms. But if you want to know what heaven looks like it's a ward in Great Ormond Street, with so much love in the ward from the doctors and nurses, so much professionalism, so much love from the parents. It's when humans give the absolute best of themselves in what is simply the worst of situations.

Great Ormond Street Hospital is a charity, and they are always in need of money. Shame on this country when they are simply not our country's priority.

Great Ormond Street was another thing that caused me to go mad. At the time I liked the fact that I could make a whole ward of kids laugh. Years later if an advert came on the telly for money for the Great Ormond Charity I would just break down in tears. A lot of that was over thirty years ago but it affected me somehow. Writing this I keep welling up in tears. Funny old world isn't it.

~ How can you spend all that time in the desert and not give the horse a name. ~

Uncle Miles

This tale is legendary in my family. I have no idea if it is true, but it has been told to me a hundred times. My Uncle Miles was supposedly the hardest man in Dublin, but most families have someone who can make this claim, or the claim is made about them. But he must have been a character. The 'Da', my grandfather, wouldn't let his sons be in the I.R.A. but Miles's best friend was Brendan Behan, who was the unofficial spokesman for the I.R.A. My own father was scared of Miles. I only met him once, at my grandmother's funeral. He didn't go to the service, he just walked in halfway through the wake, stood in the middle of the room and burst into tears.

Anyway, the story goes like this. Miles was also a brilliant pool player. There was a competition every Christmas Eve at his local when growing up and the prize was a turkey. My grandmother never had to buy a turkey at Christmas because Miles always brought one home. This particular year a load of 'Culchies' (a culchie is anyone who's Irish but doesn't come from Dublin, it's a derogatory term). I say a load because every time I'm told this story the number changes from four, five, six, eight, ten. They all challenged Miles, but he beat everyone and won the competition. He went round to shake everybody's hand but the culchies said, "We're taking the turkey", Miles says, "But that's me Ma's Turkey", and they say, "Well, we're taking it". So, Miles gets his pool cue smashes it on the table, breaks it in half and smashes the fuck out of all four, six, eight, ten culchies. A crowd gathers looking at all the blood stained people on the ground around the pool table and Miles goes to the bar to collect his prize

Now at that time the butcher still left the head and neck on the Bird with all its feathers on. Miles breaks back into the crowd, the turkey under his arm and the neck and head swinging. He goes up to the culchies points at the turkey's head swinging and says, "I told ya lads, that's me ma's turkey".

~ There are two unwritten rules in life. ~

1............

2............

My Mum

About ten years ago my mum said to me, "When I die Brendan, you'll be giving me my, what's that word?" I said, "Eulogy mum". She said "Yeah. Now don't forget I helped decorate yours and Sandra's houses". I said, "Mum, I'll give you a eulogy, and it will be more than a thanks for decorating our houses, but I'm not letting you get away with some of the things you said to me". She looked worried about this.

My mum loved Sunday mornings, she could get the roast dinner on, run down to Mass, which takes an hour, come back and the chicken and potatoes would all be done. But there was this new priest at St Joseph's Catholic Church, and his sermons went on and on and my mum felt obliged to stay till the end. She knew the roast is getting burnt because of the time this new father is taking to praise the Lord. When I asked my mum what she thought of the new priest, she said, "The trouble with him is he's too religious".

Another time, the Catholic Church was coming under a lot of scrutiny for the number of paedophiles masquerading as priests. It came out in the press that a bishop was now to be charged for the same crime. I used to tease my mum about this, although I know it's not funny. I said, "Mum the priests are at it, the bishops are at it, next we'll find out the Pope is at it".

She got me buy the scruff of the neck and said, "The priests might be at it, the bishops might be at it, but not the Pope".

She loved the Catholic Church; I asked her once if she would ever pray in a Protestant Church if she had too. She thought long and hard and said, "I would if I was desperate".

But none of that describes my mum. I remember a good friend of mine when we were growing up, Mark. His mum died when we were about twenty-one. She left him three grand, and this was quite a lot then. He coped by transferring his love onto his girlfriend and stepfather but when the money ran out, they ran out. He was now in a complete mess; I tried to help but what could I do.

One Saturday morning there's a knock on the door and it's Mark, I was pleased to see him, but he said, "I'm not here to see you Brendan, I'm here to see Helen". My mum came straight out, took one look at him, dragged him in the kitchen and told me to "Get out". At that time you didn't argue with her. I wasn't sure what was going on and I'm walking up and down the hallway, I didn't put my ear to the door, but I was sort of listening in the hall. All of a sudden, I can smell bacon, I thought 'What's going on? The sun doesn't shine brighter on anyone in this house other than me, so where's my bacon?'.

Then I hear this boo-hooing, he was crying from the very bottom of his heart. I felt embarrassed for him and nearly started crying myself. I can hear my mum consoling him. Then after a while, when all the pain had come out, she spent ages talking to him. I couldn't hear what she was saying, but I knew exactly what she was saying because I've been given that speech myself. It would have been a bollocking. "Forget about them two, just think what your mother would have said. Forget them don't be letting them upset you like this". Anyway, it went on for quite some time before he finally surfaced. He pushed past me in the hallway a new man. He walked into that flat like a sack of shit and walked out like John Wayne. My mum had done that. Who do you know, who is not family, that you can demand to see and know they will be there for you.

All my friends loved her. I remember once I had split up with a girl and was hurting. I had a friend called Teddy and he was consoling me. I told him my mum hated her, and he said, "Helen doesn't like her? Well, that'll do for me, your mum is the nicest, kindest women I have ever met and if she doesn't like her, I don't like her".

She was a terrible giggler; she very often would have fits of uncontrolled laughter, always at an inappropriate time. This one time my mum had ordered a catalogue with the latest bathroom suites, not to buy but she must have dreamed what it would be like to order a new bathroom suite. The catalogue arrived in the post, and my mum would have sat down with a cup of tea and enjoyed looking through.

What she didn't know was once you ordered the brochure you got the salesman a couple of days later. He was duly invited in and offered a cup of tea although she had no intention of buying anything. So, he starts to go through his sales pitch, and my mum would have politely listened and agreed they were lovely. Then she must have started laughing at the whole ludicrousness of this situation. About this time, I just happened to walk in, and she is in her chair giggling uncontrollably. Salesmen are told to carry on no matter what happens, this fella must have just finished the course. He opens a page of the catalogue and says, "What does Madam think of the Avocado?" My mum is literally in fits now and tries to get out, "Ahh Jesus that's lovely". The pair of us have tears running down our faces and my mum is holding her face trying not to show the tears and the laughter. After quite some time we calm down and there's a pause in the laughter. Don't forget the salesman has been told to carry on, so after this long pause, he says, "And the Pediment Blue?" We collapse in laughter; I thought I was going to die laughing.

In the end I had to intervene, I said, "Look mate this is a council flat, and she hasn't got any money" and he duly left. I had some of my best laughs with my mum.

As a kid I worked on greengrocer stalls, had to, there was no money in our house, my father was a drunk. I would go in early on a Saturday and start opening up the stall whilst the men I worked for were coming back from market with the day's produce. It was ok in the summer, but the winter mornings were dark and cold. One Saturday I was asked to go in particularly early, must have been the run up to Christmas, think I started about five in the morning. I was about fourteen; my mum was worried about me, so she followed me on her bike and stood in the street opposite me in Burton Suits doorway. When I saw her, I was so embarrassed. I was worried that all the men would come back on the lorry see my mum the other side of the street and take the piss out of me. When you're fourteen this sort of thing concerns you. So, I started shouting at her, I even told her to "Fuck off". She just ignored me and stayed there. When she thought it was light enough, and enough people were about, and I was safe she cycled off home. When I think about this now my mum has always stood across the road from me and looked out for me all through my life. It is a metaphor of course. I wish she could always be across the road looking out for me.

To pay for us kids and run a home my mum worked two jobs all her life. One was as a dinner lady in Bullers Wood School and when she had finished that job she went and cleaned a house for a rich man in a big house in Chislehurst. He and the whole family, as well as the dog, fell in love with my mum.

One day she came home and said, "That fella in the house has given me a bottle of wine, sure what do I be wanting with a bottle of wine". When I looked at it, it was a bottle of Beaujolais Nouveau, I explained that this was a new wine for this year, that the fella is obviously into his wines and has probably had a couple of crates especially flown over. This is special to him mum, it means something to him, and he has given a bottle of it to his cleaner. It's more than a bottle of wine mum. You could see she was touched.

The cross that my mother carried was she took her marriage vows in a Catholic Church, under the sight of God so they were sacred to her. She married a drunk and a ponce, but her vows said 'For better or for worse', 'For richer or for poorer' so she got the arsehole end of that deal.

As I write this my mum is suffering from severe Dementia and has lost all mobility. A couple of years ago I took her to Church on Sunday morning, she was too frail to go on her own, and so I brought her. I hadn't been in that building for years. Sat beside her and took her up to receive Holy Communion. As we were leaving, we exited down the side aisle. When a service is over the priest, father such and such, waits at the exit of the centre aisle to talk to the congregation. This poor old priest only had a couple of people queuing up to see him. This was because the whole side aisle was queuing to see my mum. Everyone wanted to talk to her and ask her how she was. It was like holding on to a celebrity or the Queen Mother. The church was full up with people that loved her. And my mum, typical of her, just wanted to tell everyone, "This is my son".

My mum politicised me without ever trying to. She was appalled at the sectarian killings and troubles in Ireland. She couldn't understand why they didn't just stop. She wrote the Good Friday Agreement long before any politician thought of it.

She hated racism. My mum came to England when bed and breakfasts had the 'No Blacks, No Dogs, No Irish' in their front room window. One time the darkies, (this was a term of endearment then) on 'Love thy Neighbour' or 'Till Death do Us Part', were really being given disgusting treatment in a series on telly one night. My mum almost had a tear in her eye and real pain in her heart when she said, "The poor old darkies, they get it awful bad". She taught me that racism is a poison.

She always cared about the underdog; she had no time for the Royal Family, she hated Thatcher for taking the free milk from children. She could never understand why they had adverts on television for animal charities when children were starving in the world. All these things influenced me in my life.

She was a strong woman. When I was little the best thing in my life was to cuddle my mum, as I grew, boys can no longer cuddle their mums, but we both missed the cuddling, so we had fights or wrestling matches. It was only when I started to develop muscles, at about seventeen that I had enough strength to beat her.

To understand the very best of my mum you had to see her when she was in company in a social environment. Certain people can 'hold court', they seem to be the centre of attention without trying. All conversation runs through them. All the laughs, the fun, the jokes, they all go through certain individuals who can hold court. When these people are on form it's a gift to be in their company. I have known certain people who can do this but the best I have ever seen by far was my mum. She was a good-looking woman, when she was buzzing, Benson and Hedges in one hand and scotch and coke in the other, she was the funniest, wittiest person I ever met. Never a lush, never slutty, never unkind, never rude, never full of herself, always bringing the quite person into the company and giving them time, always putting down the bully, always quickest with the response. There are rules to 'holding court' no one could do it better than my mum. Lessons I hope I have inherited from her.

My children have never seen this side of her, they are too young, but they would have loved to see Nanna like this. Dee my youngest daughter has inherited some of this trait.

She loved Jesus, the Catholic Church and the Pope. She never really mentioned God much.

She loved her parents, her Mammy and her Daddy.

She loved her brothers and sisters, Olive, Miles, Mick, Pat, Willie, Mary, and Betty all have a special place in her heart.

She may have loved her husband when she was young but this waned.

She married a man, and her parents didn't go to their wedding, and her son didn't go to his funeral, I think this speaks volumes.

She loved her time with her children when they were young. This was the best time off her life.

She loved the fact that she got to do it all again with her grandchildren.

She loved me the most, if I shot the Pope, she would have said, "Don't worry son, they'll get another one". I have not got the words, intellect or talent to write down how much I love her, enough said.

~ Love you Mum. ~

Another Crane Story

1980's London Euston, get called to a woman up a crane threatening to jump. When we turned up, we could make out a girl sitting on the counter balancing concrete weights on one end of the crane. She seemed miles away, really high up, so Chris Connelly and I started climbing up the crane via the built in Jacob's Ladder. We got to where the two arms of the crane go out, and I started to head out to her. I walked through the centre of the triangle of steel. I say walked; I had to walk across the cable and pulleys that the cable runs on. This was all covered in grease to make it run better, so I had my hands on the top part of the triangular steel holding on and slipping over the cables. We are miles up in the sky. I thought 'Jesus'.

I get out to her after some time, and she is just sitting on the edge of the concrete weights trying to work up the courage to jump. She is just trying to push herself off but the instinct for survival built into us is strong. She sees me and tells me to 'Fuck off', that if I come near her, she will jump. I was absolutely shitting myself. I said, "I'm not going to come anywhere near you, if I do, we will both go over the side, and I don't want to die tonight". Then she just keeps telling me to

'Fuck off and leave her alone'. I explained "I can't go, it's my job, I have to stay here".

After some sort of Mexican standoff, I said, "Look I'm fucking frightened, can we just calm down". Somehow, she agreed to this, so she's sat one end of the concrete blocks, I'm sat on the other end, no harness covered in grease. We sat there for about half an hour just looking out over the London skyline, somehow it seemed quite nice. I didn't have a clue what to do next but said out loud "I could kill a fag". She said, "So could I", so I made some sort of a connection. I radioed Chris who was waiting back at the cross tree of arms and asked him if he had any fags on him, he said he did. Then she said, "If anyone else comes out here I will jump". So, I said "Alright, I'll go and get them". So the poxy slipping and sliding starts again as I go back to Chris Connelly to get the fags.

I finally make my way back out to her, sit down in my spot, light her a fag and pass it at arm's length. This somehow breaks the ice and we start talking.

She told me that she was a heroin addict. That the authorities had taken her child away, that she had been made homeless, and that there was no point in living anymore and she wanted to end it.

At that time aids was rife amongst drug users, and I remember thinking don't say you've got aids because

I thought you might as well jump. Anyway, she didn't say that.

We sat there just chatting for hours. I even made her laugh a couple of times. In the end we both just come to the conclusion that things will get better, that she's a mother and she had to come down and face all this. And she agreed to come down. So, the pair of us are like Torvil and Dean, slipping and sliding back to the ladder.

When we got to the bottom of the crane the police and medical people grabbed hold of her, injected her with some sort of sedative and took her away. I remember thinking there was no need for this type of treatment as she had agreed to come down herself. I kind of got a bit angry about it. Then Chris says to me, "You're getting involved, your job's done. Forget it" I realised he was right, and we all went back to the station.

At that time, I was in a partnership with Neil Whinstone. We done property, buying and selling houses. Bromley and Kentish Times, Bromley's local paper had got hold of the story and wanted to come and interview me the next day. I was on a job with Neil when they turned up, He loved it. I made the front page, headline 'Fireman Brendan Hailed as a Hero'. This was before 'Social media', everyone read papers then. I was Bromley's celebrity for the week. Still have the press cutting.

~ Don't walk in front of me I might forget you,

Don't walk behind me I might lose my way

Just walk beside me and be my friend. ~

Dogs

When I was a kid, we used to get a Red Bus Rover ticket. For twenty-five pence you could buy a bus ticket that let you ride on any bus that day. They were the old Routemaster busses, so you could jump on and off any time you wanted and at any place, you didn't have to wait at the bus stop. We would get the forty-seven up to London and jump on and off the buses all day. It was great fun.

One day we've ended up in Petticoat Lane Street Market. It was a great market; it sold everything and anything, records, clothes and animals. You could buy puppies and kittens. I saw this little black puppy and came home with it. My mum went mad and had nothing to do with it. Then it cut its paw on some glass and was hurting and my mum nursed it back to health. From then on, she was attached to it. It became Tony the Dog and became a legend.

I was over the park walking it one day, when it was still a puppy, and this fighting dog, not sure of the breed, came running over and attacked it. It had it in its mouth and was ripping the shit out of it and Tony was barking in that high pitched tone, almost a scream. I went to kick it as hard as I could and missed and pulled the ligaments in my leg. I'm now hopping around, Tony is screaming and I done what you should never do, I put my hand between two dogs fighting. This fighting dog, with its strengthened jaw, bit the tip of my finger off. I can't walk properly; blood is pissing out of my finger and Tony's still screaming. It was one of the most harrowing times of my life. Finally, the owner gets hold of his dog, I pick Tony up and limp home covering us both in blood and got taken to hospital.

I had to have a skin graft. The doctors took skin from behind my bicep and stitched it on the top of my finger. The top of my finger looked like a ragdoll, where they just stitch the leather up to make it look like a shoe. I remember feeling ok until the injections wore off. I was given pain killers by the doctors, but they didn't work, the pain was the worst I had personally ever felt. Until Mary broke my heart at seventeen.

Afterwards, because I'd pulled the ligaments in my leg so bad, I was given a crutch to help me walk. I had my arm bandaged where they'd taken the skin from my arm, my finger bandaged and my whole arm in a sling. I looked like I'd just come back from a war. When people saw me, they would say in shock, "What's happened to you" I would reply, "A dog bit me" and they would say, "Fuck me it must have been a big dog".

Both my parents are Irish, all four of my grandparents are Irish, all eight of my great grandparents are Irish, I can't be English, even though I was born in England. I have noticed to be English you have to love dogs and you have to love the Royal Family. I don't, I love children. I sit in amazement when I see a young woman with a baby in her pram, and a dog on a lead, and English people walk up to the young woman and ask the dog's name and totally ignore the baby. It's a dog, that's a child in the pushchair. They are oblivious to this young child and just want to stroke 'Tiddles'. This would never happen in Ireland, or indeed Spain or Italy or anywhere but England.

Anyway, back to dog stories. Pulled up to a fire and the bottom four houses are well alight. Flames and smoke pouring out the ground floor windows. Two floors up there are people leaning out of every window trapped. The fire brigade was at its professional best that night, I was proud to be a part of it. Ladders were pitched and rescues started happening, all the people were brought down safely. Jets (hoses) were laid out, firefighters went in, and the fires were going out. Everything was just happening like it should. I was driving the fire engine that night, but the fire was on another fire ground, so my role in that situation was to assist the other driver to set into the hydrant, so he doesn't run out of water. As you can imagine, he was quite busy.

While I'm doing this, I notice there is a great big alsatian with his paws on the window on the second-floor barking with all the excitement. There is an old man next to him who is obviously the priority. The ladder had been pitched to get the old boy down; we were set into the hydrant. Everything seemed under control, so I thought; I'm going to get that dog down.

What wasn't happening was this, the fireman who had gone up to get the old boy was taking too long to get him down. You assist people down a ladder in that situation; cradle them in your arms. But most of the time you have to bully them, because they're so frightened about leaving the building and getting on the ladder. You make them more frightened of you than the fire. I don't know if the firefighter was a recruit, but he was taking way too long to get him down. I'm waiting at the bottom of the ladder to run up and grab this dog. Two police dog handlers had turned up and were also concerned about this alsatian, I said, "Don't worry lads, as soon as he gets him down, I'm on it". I think they gave me a dog harness.

After what seemed like an eternity the fireman brings him down. The dog's barking had changed from excitement to concern as the flames and smoke were getting hotter. I ran up the ladder but the fire and smoke was now punching out of the window. The Alsatian was no longer at the window. I leant over the windowsill to see if I could feel him, but the fire was now leaking out at the top of the window and burning my neck. I shit myself and pulled myself back. I remember thinking it isn't worth dying for. I climbed down, said, "Sorry" to the police who were upset by it, and they said, "Don't worry, we could see you tried your best".

When the fire was out, I went back upstairs and this great big alsatian was lying underneath the window, dead as a dodo, it made me feel sad. Later I thought to myself, suppose that had been a little child, how would you feel now.

Another thing the English do is they say "My dog is my child" as though this is somehow true. I have known people who have lost children, something in them dies, and they are never the same person again. They might appear to be okay a couple of years later, but if you delve deeper, they're not, they are never the same.

I know it hurts if your dog dies, I cried when we lost Tony the Dog. But you get over the death of a dog very quickly.

I remember a fireman came to work one night and he obviously wasn't right. During dinner someone said, "What's up with you?" and he blubbed out, "My poxy dog has died, seventeen years I had him" and started crying his eyes out. It was sad but we all just burst out laughing. There was a fireman on the watch who was a big Elvis fan, and he could sing like him. He got on the Tannoy system and started singing 'Old Shep'. We were pissing ourselves. In the end the fireman who had lost his dog stated laughing. That wouldn't have happened if he had lost a child.

There's also this myth that a dog loves you. It doesn't. A dog is a pack animal, stop feeding it and see how you get on. I have been called, on more than one occasion, to a smell coming from an elderly person's flat. When you gain access, the old lady has died and has fallen on the floor. This may have happened two months ago. Her little pet dog has started starving to death, so it eats the old lady. It will start with the exposed flesh. The nose, ears, lips, and face. When that meat has gone it will start on her legs or arms. This rotting flesh is now covered in maggots; hence the smell, and we get called. Little 'Tiddles' has done nothing wrong; it's an animal and was starving. It doesn't 'love' its master. The master is its food provider.

I'm in my sixties and single and sometimes end up on the 'broken dreams' dating sites. At my age a lot of women have raised their children, sent them off to university or a relationship, and now have a void in their life. So, they get a dog to fill this void. This never works; a dog cannot replace human relationships, so they go on a dating site. I end up buying them a coffee, not realising I will always come second to the dog.

I was seeing this one girl from Guilford. I quite liked her and after the obligatory third date I was going to spend the night. We went upstairs and started to strip off, laid on the bed and started kissing. You've all been here. Then her dog jumps on the bed, makes itself combatable and starts staring at me. I said, "What's going on?" she said, "Oh ignore him he sleeps with me". I said, "If I didn't wash, or clean my teeth, or wipe my feet, or clean my arse, and greeted other people by sticking my nose up someone else's arse, who also didn't wipe their arse, would you let me in your bed?". She said "No". "So why are you letting that thing do it?". She said, "It's different". I got dressed and went home.

When I was a kid playing in the park, you constantly trod in dog shit. A large part of your childhood then was cleaning dog shit off your shoe. Thank God that has stopped. But worse than having to clean dog shit off my shoe would be the indignation of running after a dog when it's having a shit and then picking this up. It's simply disgusting, how do people do that? I could never have that in my life.

If you want a good laugh, watch an intelligent dog having a shit. Then watch it looking at its master as it picks up the shit. You can see the dog thinking 'What do you want that for, that's shit'.

The last thing I have to say about dogs is fighting dogs. How is this allowed? In England you hear all the time 'It's not the dog's fault it's the owners.' This is absolute rubbish, fighting dogs are wired to attack, they're bred for this specific task. But because of the English obsession with dogs, we allow them to walk freely where children play, in parks, playgrounds, etc. You even hear of young families with children having fighting dogs in the same house, and they end up attacking the children. It is unpopular for MPs to legislate against dogs in this country, this has to change. Enough said.

~ If the shoes don't fit, they ain't your shoes. Homer Simpson 1984. ~

Neil Winstone

I have a friend, has been for years, Neil Whinstone. He was my best man at my wedding and years ago we had a building company together. 'French Construction', Neil wanted to use the name 'French' as it looked so good on our cards we had made up, with the French tricolour printed on them.

In a world full of bland people Neil is a character, he can be really funny and good company. He, like me, is a raconteur, loves to tell a story. He can hold court. Oh, and he loves animals. The stories I tell about Neil all involve animals.

He was driving once down a country lane in winter, it was pissing down, and he sees a dead sheep in the road that had been hit by a car. Neil felt sorry for the poor bugger so he tried to drag it out of the road up on the bank so it wouldn't get hit by anymore cars. You've got to imagine the scene, it's dark, it's raining, the bank is all wet and slippery and Neil is struggling to get this sheep up on the bank. All of a sudden, a bloke pulls up in a Rolls Royce, undoes his electric window and says, "Driving too fast, were we?"

He once got a dog from a rescue centre. I remember him telling me, he was all full of it about his new dog and how lovely he was. When Neil took it over the park and a black person turned up the dog started attacking them, the previous owner had trained it to be a 'white' dog. Black people would look at him in disgust; this racist has trained his dog to be a white dog. And Neil would start apologising explaining that he got it from a rescue centre.

Another story, he had just bought an expensive car. B.M.W. or Mercedes Estate, can't remember which one. While he's driving down a country lane he sees a goat in the road. Anyone else would just drive by, but not Neil. He captures it, puts it in the boot of his new estate car and drives it to Christmas Tree Farm. This was a little small holding where the public could pay to go in and feed all the sheep and pigs and goats. I've had great fun there with my kids.

Anyway, the goat starts kicking and ramming the fuck out of Neil's new car. It's frightened and it's trapped, and it just wants out, so it's just kicking and ramming everything it can to get out.

Neil finally gets it to Christmas Tree Farm, and the man comes out. Neil tells him that he found it in the road and brought it here for safety. Then this fella says, "You can't bring that in here, that's a billy goat it will cause havoc with all the other goats". So Neil says, "What should I do?" And the man says, "Bring it back where you found it, the farmer will soon get it".

So, Neil puts the billy goat back in his car and drives it back to where he found it, and the kicking and the ramming the fuck out of Neil's car starts all over again. Cost him over a thousand pound.

But the best Neil story is this one.

The new M23 had just been built, this is the road from London to Brighton and Neil was using it a lot for work. He noticed that there were a lot of dead badgers on the side of the new motorway. This appalled Neil, and he wrote a letter to the Croydon Express that the proper badger tunnels hadn't been put in.

Badger setts are amongst the oldest occupied habitats in the country. Some date back to Norman times and the routes that badgers take, 'badger trails', are just as old. Some construction company had built a motor way right over them and Neil wasn't taking this lying down.

So, the letter to the paper kicked off a little mini campaign with other people writing in, in agreement. Low and behold the construction company gets hold of Neil and asks him to come to their headquarters to discuss the issue.

Neil turns up in a suit thinking he is going to be sweet talked into some kind of compromise, a bit of a champagne event. But as soon as he gets there, he's given a fluorescent jacket, a pair of wellington boots, stuck in an old dirty diesel van, and driven up and down the new M23. They ask Neil where they should put the new tunnels. Neil by now is in too deep. He's too embarrassed to say "I don't fucking know" so he starts telling them where to put the new tunnels.

It cost this construction company millions and made no difference to the amount of badgers getting killed.

~ He was a really good best man, humiliated me terrible. I have always hoped he would get married so I can return the favour. ~

IVF

In Vitro Fertilization (I.V.F.) is a process of fertilization where the egg is combined with a sperm 'In vitro'.

Sarah and I were happily married, worth a few bob, cracking on with our lives, careers, everything was good. Sarah early thirties, me nearly forty, so we decided the next logical thing to do was have children. And we both wanted them.

We didn't make a big thing of this at first; our form of contraception was to pull it out, the withdrawal method. From then on, we decided to leave it in. Nothing happened and the nothingness got louder and louder as time went on.

We started to book up the ideal time to get pregnant, five days before ovulation. At first Sarah would dress up in sexy underwear, but in the end this seemed pointless. We weren't having 'sex' we were trying to make babies, my job was to just do the deed, and it wasn't sexy. I ended up hating these nights, the stress of having to perform. When a man gets like this it's impossible to get an erection. Our 'nights' became a farce.

But it simply would not happen. Every time Sarah would have a period she would start screaming and we would end up arguing. I understood how Sarah was feeling, she felt her body clock was running out, that she wouldn't become a mother. But the stress of the whole thing at that time was horrendous. I ended up hating having to go home and try and have sex. It was nobody's fault.

Anyway, after about eighteen months of this we decided to try I.V.F. We booked into a private clinic under Ms Hanna. I had to give a sperm sample, so duly turned up, embarrassed as hell, to give my sperm. I was taken into a room by a junior doctor. It was a plain empty room except for a couple of chairs and before the doctor left he gives me a folder. I looked in amazement; I thought it was instructions on how to have a wank. I remember thinking I don't need that son I'm an expert at it. But I took it and he left. When I opened this folder, it had an old Playboy magazine in it from the seventies and some of the pages were stuck together, presumable from previous patients. I felt as horny as a monk taking a cold shower. I tried but nothing was happening, the ole fella said, "Sorry mate not interested" and I went back to reception. They said, "Don't worry, this often happens, take this container and do it at home place it under your armpit and bring it straight to us". This was duly done, and I came back with a transparent little tub, and everyone could see it was full of my sperm. Sarah went in to give her eggs, and we waited for the news.

Eureka it worked, thank God, if it hadn't of Christ knows how Sarah would have reacted. They told us they had a really good fertile egg to put back, and they had some spare ones which they would put in as backup. You just listen at this stage, you don't know enough to have an opinion.

So then we get booked in to have the fertile eggs put back in. This was amongst the most clinical part of the whole process. Sarah is lying on an operating table with her legs in stirrups, wide apart. I felt her embarrassment. I'm in an operating gown standing next to her. We've all got masks and hats on, and the doctor has got a syringe in his rubber gloved hands, with a long length of fibreglass bouncing around. He's just about to insert this into Sarah and the nurse turns the lights down and plays Lionel Ritchie's 'Your Once, Twice, Three Times a Lady', to try and make this, the time of conception, romantic. I thought Jesus. It was good of them to try, but it didn't work, this was not romantic it was just clinical.

We then had to wait until it was time for a scan. Sarah was brilliant at this time, no smoking, no drinking, and eating all the right foods. We get the call; it's time for the scan. Go in and they rub this jelly on Sarah's stomach and start searching for a baby. It's worked, there's this great big heart beating, it was obviously Dan. Obviously I was happy, but my main thoughts were, 'Thank fuck for that', if they had found nothing the stress and the shouting would have been unbearable. Then all of a sudden, the nurse says, "Hold on a minute, there's another one" and you could see this little heart beating, about half the size of Dan's, it seemed to be struggling to stay alive. I fell in love with it there and then. I loved Dan's just as much, but he didn't seem to need much help. Then the nurse says, "Do you want us to take it out to give the other one a better chance?" I immediately thought, anyone touches that child, I'll kill them, leave it alone. I didn't care what anyone said but Sarah being Sarah totally agreed and said, "No, leave it". She had already fallen in love with it as well. When we got home the relief was incredible, for Sarah, me and our parents. Thank God for that.

By the time it was time they came out, Sarah was huge. Sarah was induced so we both turned up when they thought the time was ready. I had already been through a birth with Chloe so this time I knew to stay away from the sharp end, I don't think there's any need for a man to watch a birth. It was a caesarean section birth so they both came out quite easily. This will always be the biggest thing that happens in your life, anyone's life. To see your child, covered in blood and guts, wriggling and screaming is the most amazing thing you will ever see.

So they're getting cleaned up and weighed and I'm over looking at them and I couldn't get my head around that there was two of them. I, of course knew we were getting twins, but to see two babies was amazing. But something else was happening, the doctors went professional. I have seen enough people under trains, getting cut out of cars or other emergencies to know when the medics are losing them. Sarah had passed out, and the doctors went quiet. When this happens, they don't waste words, they only talk in this doctor word speak, they concentrate, all the joy leaves their faces. I could see they were losing her. My emotions now have never been so fucked up. I'm looking at two babies and feel as happy as can be but also looking at Sarah and thinking she might die. Getting these two big buggers out has taken its toll and it might kill her.

I then start thinking what will I do if Sarah doesn't make it. I started thinking Sally, Sarah's mum will have to move in with me. That Sarah wanted this thing so badly and now she won't see it. So, I'm holding these babies, shouting out in my head "Come on Sarah". After what seemed an eternity, she comes round and the doctors start smiling again, thank God.

Now I get to do a wonderful thing that every dad gets to do. You take the babies out to the grandparents. I took one of them; I don't know which one and put it in Sally's arms. I think you should go to the mum's mum first, but the good thing was we had two of the buggers so I could go and get the other one and give it to my mum. Brilliant, both grandmothers had a baby to hold.

So, babies cuddled and put down to sleep, Sarah resting and grandparents all happy and gone home, I went down the cafe. As I'm driving down U2 are playing 'It's a Beautiful Day' on the radio. Enough said.

~ Look after the birds, and the bees, and the trees, and the seas. ~

The Marchioness

1989, Euston Fire Station, got a call to a pleasure boat hit by another boat, River Thames, Southwark Bridge. When we got there, we couldn't see anything looking over the bridge, there was just this one man pointing at the Thames. He was in a complete state, he couldn't talk properly, and he's acting like a mad person. But there was nothing to look at where he is pointing. So, we just thought 'nutter'. Different information was gathered and slowly it emerged that a pleasure boat, The Marchioness had been hit by a much bigger boat, The Bow Bell, a Dredger, and had sunk. The Marchioness was full of young people, party goers, having a night on a disco boat. The boat had indeed been hit by where we were standing but the tide had carried her up stream. The poor man had witnessed this and that was why he was in a complete state.

Fifty-one young people died that night and it was one of the biggest tragedies on the Thames. A lot of families were left devastated and court cases and inquires followed. But that's not my story, tragically that's their story. My story is this.

After a time, the fire brigade in attendance was ordered to get a ceiling hook, this is a long pole with a blade-come-hook on the end, they're carried on every fire engine, mainly to pull down fire damaged ceilings, and to go to the bottom of the bridges along the Thames. There is normally a platform where the bridge goes into the water. So, our crew were standing on the platform of one of the bridges and checking for dead bodies that might be floating up the Thames as the tide was heading up stream. There were a few police helicopters flying above aiming their search lights down at the water.

All of a sudden we heard this whoo, whoo, whoo noise and it was getting louder and we all wondered what it was, it was quite frightening. Then this massive Sea King helicopter comes over the bridge and is so near to us we could see the pilot's eyes. The wind that comes off these things nearly knocked you off your feet, we had to hold onto the rail to stand up and now the whoo-whooing was going right through your body. There were loads of lights coming off this thing. It felt like you were next to the spaceship in 'Close Encounters of the Third Kind'.

There was a crew member at the door on the side, he was clipped on, and we could see he had radio communication with the pilot. From the way he was animated, and his arm signals you can see that he's telling the pilot to get lower. The blades of this helicopter are about a meter away from the bridge and the crew member keeps telling him to get lower. You could see real concern in the pilot's face and we're thinking if he gets this wrong, we've probably all had it. He finally gets the crew member low enough to pick up this piece of debris. He realises it is nothing and they fly off to look somewhere else.

I have never witnessed anything as awe inspiring as that helicopter pilot. His bravery and skill are the best I have ever witnessed at any operational situation. We were all silenced by what we had just witnessed. I cannot praise his skill enough, amazing. We are so lucky in this country to have all the emergency services, and I do mean all, which are full of personnel that put their lives on the line to help others.

~ I spent all my money on wine, women, and song, and like a fool I wasted the rest. ~

Irish Instructions

The Irish have a gift for giving instructions for telling you where to go. English instructions are specific; they leave no room for misinterpretation. Irish instructions are more poetic, more a way of life. When asking my Uncle Noel, who is a very intelligent man, how to drive to Grafton Street in Dublin, he said, "Follow the main road to Dublin, go straight over four sets of traffic lights, on the fifth set take a left, or is it a right? I'm not sure. Ah you'll know when you get there". Another time when I asked an Irish gentleman for instructions, he said, "Go straight down to the roundabout, if you take the first left, that will take you to St Mary's Church, don't go down there. If you take the next left, that's where my Aunt Maggie used to live, God rest her soul, don't go down there. If you go straight on, you'll end up in Phoenix Park, don't go straight on. But if you take the next left (which is a right in England), that'll get you there". Only in Ireland!

I remember seeing my Uncle Willie once and he said to me, "Wait 'til you hear this one". He had bumped into an old mate from work, who he hadn't seen for years, and the friend invited him to his son's wedding, next week. He told him, "The wedding is at Our Ladies Church on Saturday, at midday, and the reception is at that big pub in Ballyfermot, I can't think of the name of it, but you'll know it when you get there". An Irish instruction has now been given.

He went with his wife Colette, and my Uncle Mick, I loved Mick, he was a real no nonsense man. So, there was three of them in the car. Now if you're Irish and you have a spare seat in the car, you offer a lift to anyone who needs it. So, after the service Willie offered a lift to anyone who needed it. This one woman had to make her own way to the reception, so she duly accepted.

When Willie pulled up at the big pub in Ballyfermot, it was empty, he asked the barman about the reception, he said it wasn't here, but he thinks there's one at the pub a couple of miles down the road on the right. Another Irish instruction has been given. When they get to the suggested pub it's the same response. So, they start driving all over Dublin trying to find the reception getting new Irish instructions as they go.

All of a sudden, the woman who had taken the lift, her phone rings and the conversation goes like this. (Do it in Irish accent) "Maggie where are ya?" "I don't where the fuck I am, these fucking ejits haven't a fucking clue where they are. The fucking stupid bastards have me lost". So, my Uncle Mick, who is sat next to her says, "Willie throw her out, fuck her off out of it". The woman says, "Throw me out? Yous cunts offered me a fucking lift, if I'd of known yous were fucking ejits, I wouldn't have got in". My Uncle Mick, "Throw her out at the fucking lights".

My Uncle Willie who is driving said he was pissing himself with laughter. He had tears rolling down his face telling me the story. Anyway, they finally find the pub. When they pull up the woman gets out and with two hands on the door slams it shut as hard as she can and storms off.

All during the evening there are devils looks from the woman if their eyes meet, but a good time was had anyway and the evening come to an end. Now they have to drive back to Crumlin and if you're Irish and there's a spare seat in the car you offer a lift. This is just instinctive, but as Willie is saying it, his eyes catch the woman, who is staring at him, and she says to him "Fuck off".

~ Paddy gets out of the Airport in New York, and a black fella comes up to him and says,

"Do you want to buy some shit man?"

Paddy says, "Do I want to buy some shit!"

"It's good shit man"

"It's good shit? Tell me where have you got this shit?"

"Got it right here in my pocket man"

"You've shit in your fucking pocket". ~

God Needs a Dentist

I needed a new dentist; the fire brigade paid your dental charges then, but only National Health dentist charges. Even then, and this was the nineties, it was becoming increasingly hard to find a National Health dentist. So a friend put me on to Mark Spurway and gave me his phone number. When I contacted him, he told me his practice was in Harley Street, this is the main street in London for all things medical, it's world renowned and all private. I told him my situation and that I needed a National Health receipt because then I get it free. He said that's not a problem, but I would have to go to his clinic in Streatham. This was duly booked up.

When I turned up, I found out that Mark paid for this practice out of his own money. The rent, the rates, all the equipment, the staff, everything he paid for himself, and it ran at a huge loss. He knew he was in a position of privilege, working in Harley Street, in his private practice, earning huge amounts of money and wanted to put something back into the community. This was his way of doing it.

I got to know him quite well; I went there for years and got along with all the staff. It was always interesting going because it seemed every vagabond, homeless, desperate person turned up there to have their teeth sorted out. I remember once I had been waiting about half an hour for my appointment and there was this black fella holding his mouth in pain. He looked really desperate. Mark came out and said, "Sorry Brendan, I'm going to have to deal with him first". This I understood. The fella came out about an hour later with Mark and he just looked so relived. There was a cabinet on the wall full of toothpaste and brushes and floss, Mark got a big handful of stuff from the cabinet and just gave it to him. No money was asked for, nothing was signed, he was just helped for free. He became a hero of mine; it was like my dentist was a real Che Guevara, and we became friends.

His passion in life was scuba diving; his favourite thing to do was to go to the Red Sea and scuba dive. He went one time and drowned and that was the end of him. I went back to the dentist, but it closed not long after he passed. I saw the girl on reception. She knew I heard about it and looked at me, welled up and said, "God needed a dentist".

~ I went to the dentist once and he said, "Your teeth are alright, but your gums have got to come out". ~

Rolf Harris

I grew up with Rolf Harris on the telly. I watched him paint, they were really good paintings, you could never tell what he was painting until the very last brush stroke. He would keep teasing you saying, "Can you see what it is yet?" Then, finally it was revealed, a koala would be climbing up a tree. It was brilliant. He taught me to swim. He had a swimming lesson show every Saturday morning. Neither of my parents could swim, so he taught me about breathing technique and the different strokes. We learnt about the didgeridoo, the boomerang, and the little joey in a kangaroo's pouch. The Rolf Harris television special was not to be missed.

He also had hit after hit record, every one of my generation can sing them all. 'Sun Arise Come in The Morning', 'Jake the Peg', 'Tie your Kangaroo Down Sport' and his most famous, 'Two Little Boys'. Some of these songs competed with the Beatles for the number one spot.

I was driving once, in the early eighties and Rolf Harris was a guest on the Terry Wogan morning radio show. He told a story as to why 'Two Little Boys' meant so much to him. His grandmother or great grandmother, on his mother's side, I think, had two sons. One was fifteen and the other fourteen.

They had joined up to fight with the Anzacs (Australian and New Zealand Army Corps). To go and fight in Gallipoli against the Turks. You had to be seventeen to serve in this corps.

When the mother heard what they had done she dragged them both back and demanded they wasn't allowed to go. The Sergeant Major said, "It's too late the paperwork has been singed". But she pleaded with him and said, "You can have the fifteen-year-old but not the fourteen-year-old". Eventually the Sergeant Major agreed and the fifteen-year-old went off to war and the fourteen-year-old went home.

Now, the thing about these two boys is the older brother was a 'mush' he could handle himself; he could have a fight; he knew how to take care of himself. The sort of man you knew wouldn't get killed in a war. The younger brother, the 'runt', wasn't like that; he relied on his older brother to take care of him. After eighteen months the younger brother was considered old enough to join up, his mother couldn't stop him any longer. So, he joined but was sent to a different regiment.

The older brother came back without a scratch on him. The younger brother came up against a Turk's machine gun and didn't come back.

For the rest of her life the mother wished she had let them both go together. She knew the older brother would have taken care of the younger brother. The 'mush' would have brought the 'runt' home.

As Rolf Harris is telling this story to Terry Wogan he starts crying his eyes out on the radio, Terry Wogan is crying and I'm crying so much I had to pull the car over because I couldn't drive. It then leads into 'Two Little Boys' and you could see other people crying in their cars.

We then found out Rolf Harris was a paedophile, and we couldn't like him anymore. Rolf, you stole my childhood.

~ I bought a didgeridoo once from a charity shop and tried to learn to play it. I thought I best check with my neighbour that it wasn't too loud. When I knocked on the door to ask him, he said, "NoooooooooooOhoooooooooooooOhooooo". ~

Arse

I love words; so much can be said with words (pardon the pun). Words can make you cry, make you laugh, make you think, change your whole world. But the most amazing thing about words is they all come from 26 little letters. Think of all the works of Shakespeare, he only used 26 letters. Great authors: Hemingway, Lee, and Orwell all only used 26 letters. George Orwell used the 26 letters so well they named a style of writing after him, 'Orwellian'. But I think the most amazing word of all is, 'arse', your buttocks, it can mean so much. Let me explain.

Dumb Arse - Limited intelligent.

Smart Arse - Very intelligent or thinks their intelligent.

Fat Arse - A person who is overweight.

Short Arse - A short person.

Lazy Arse - A person who is lazy.

Bad Arse - A person who is violent or street smart.

Lard Arse - A fat person.

Tight Arse - A person who is mean, especially with money.

Half Arsed - Someone who never really commits to anything.

Piece of Arse - A sexy woman.

My Arse - A person who doesn't care about a situation.

Kiss my Arse - A person who is glad to be out of a situation or goodbye.

Arsehole - Showing disdain for an individual.

What an Arse - Calling someone stupid.

Pompous Arse - Someone who is full of their own importance.

Move your Arse - Asking someone to move or work faster.

Can't be Arsed - Not interested in doing anything.

Arse bandit - A person of ill dispute or gay person.

An Arse - An idiot.

Arse cheek - One half of your buttocks.

Arse crack - The line between your two buttock checks.

Arse end - The wrong end.

Arse up - The wrong way up.

A pain in the Arse - An annoying person.

Arse kissing - Flattery to gain favour.

Arse about face - The wrong way round.

Get your Arse into gear - To do or start something seriously.

He can't tell his Arse from his elbow - Failure to understand situation.

Arse around - To act stupid.

Kicked Arse - To beat an opponent or do well.

Get off your Arse - Start to do something.

Up his own Arse - Full of themselves, pretentious.

Arseholed - Very drunk.

Talking out of your Arse - To talk foolishly.

Arse over Tit - To fall uncontrollably.

Head up his Arse - Doesn't grasp the situation or aloof.

Freeze my Arse off - To be really cold.

Laughed my Arse off - To laugh a lot.

Worked my Arse off - To work a lot.

Out on your Arse - Unconscious or defeated.

Arse licker - A sycophantic person.

Ducks Arse - A complete mess up or teddy boy's haircut.

Up the Arse - Anal sex.

Stick it up your Arse - I'm simply not doing it.

You're like my bum, your only an Arse – Disdain.

My fanny is chewing my Arse off - A very horny girl.

See what I mean, 'Arse' is actually slang for buttocks. Love is the most important word in the English language, but it seems to me 'Arse' means everything.

~ I don't care if you don't agree with me; stick it up your arse. ~

Mediterranean Mooring

In England we have tides. The difference between high tide and low tide at springs is immense. The highest tides that come every two weeks, can be up to four meters; therefore, if you tied up to the dock or shore at high tide, the boat would be hanging on its lines at low tide. The way we get over this is to tie up to pontoons. These are floating decks that move up and down with the tide, they are secured to metal pylons that are sunk into the ground. Most pleasure boats in Britain are moored like this, with the boats side tied up to the pontoon.

Tides are much more negligible in the Med. This is because the bottom of Spain and the top of Africa are very close together and do not let the flow from the Atlantic through. By the time the water gets up to the eastern Med the difference between high tide and low tide can be as little as eight inches. This allows boats to be tied up to the dock or quayside at their stern, or rear, with a line from the bows, or front, to a secure fixing in the sea. This is called 'Med mooring'.

Brits abroad seem to have trouble with this kind of mooring and panic will very often ensue. The manoeuvre is very simple, but then I've done it thousands of times. Preparation is key, fenders out either side, two stern lines, port and starboard, that's two lines left and right at the back of the boat, ready to be passed to the dock master or someone who knows what they're doing. Reverse in slowly, pass your stern lines to the person on the dock. Take the shoreline, go to the front of the boat, and tie off to the line tied to the bottom of the sea. Simple. The boat is now secured fore and aft. Back and front. But as I say, this seems to cause so much panic time and time again.

My ex-wife Sarah was never comfortable sailing; she didn't like it. She was never confident, and because of this, rows can start very easily. Every time we pulled in somewhere she would panic and start shouting, this can't happen, so we agreed she would stay below and I would moor the boat on my own, it was just easier.

We bought a boat in Croatia, a thirty-eight-foot Bavaria sailboat, when the twins were about a year old, and spent a summer sailing around the islands of Croatia, it was brilliant. I would strap Dan and Dee's buggy on the deck near where I would steer from and then strap them in the buggy. They loved it, sitting like a King and Queen on their throne surveying all around them, as we sailed around Croatia.

But of course, every evening we had to moor up at another beautiful Croatian Island; c 'est la vie. So, Sarah stayed below and I moored up on my own. But now I had to get the twins off the boat, and this was over the passerelle. This sounds posh, but in most cases it's a scaffold board from the back of the boat to the dock, it was on mine. The first time I did this I wasn't sure how it could be done without losing the kids over the side, so I was worried. Then I noticed two old ladies sitting on a bench.

The Med is full of old ladies, normally dressed in black with wrinkled skin from too much time in the sun. They were beautiful young women once, they have been brides, mothers, grandmothers but are now widowed and all the family has grown and fled. Their life has no real purpose now, so they gather down by the water to pass the time away.

Anyway, I grab one of the twins, take it up the plank and plonk it on one of these old ladies' laps. After the initial shock she loved it, for one thing they are an expert in is babies. I then went and got the other one and plonked it on the other free lap. They were both in heaven, Dan and Dee loved it as well, all the attention. I could now carry the buggy up the plank and put the kids back in it, thanking the women, but there was no need. They could only speak Croatian, and I could only speak English, but we connected. Sarah would now come up, attire and makeup sorted and discover the new town.

This happened in 2004 when Croatia was still a young country. The Balkan war was a near memory. It was still very parochial, tourism was relatively new, so all the islanders knew each other. Word passed on the grapevine, or should I say mooring line. When we pulled up at the next island there were four old ladies waiting to get hold of one of the twins. twins are very special in Croatia and word had got round, if you were lucky you got to hold one. And so, it went on, any time we were sailing around there was a crowd of old ladies waiting at the dock to hold a twin. It really was a special time.

~ All relationship are bank accounts, if you keep putting in and get nothing back, close it down. ~

Nigel Farage

My part in his success

I cannot prove this next anecdote is factually correct. I will tell it as it factually happened to me, but I'm not claiming it to be true 'beyond all reasonable doubt'.

I was on a union course, 'Media Training'. The course was run by a woman; I do not remember her name. She was so forthright, powerful, and professional. She spoke with real authority, the type of person that when they speak, you listen.

It was said that she put Milbank together. This was the press liaison headquarters for 'New Labour', when Tony Blair was at his most powerful. It was taken over by Alistair Campbell who ran it with a rod of iron. Its main purpose, the left always came across in the press as foolish, disjointed and not singing from the same hymn sheet. Some Labour MPs would say they believe in a nuclear deterrent, others would say they want it scrapped. Others would say we must spend our way out of a recession whilst the Chancellor would insist on fiscal prudence. If you have ever heard Diane Abbott go off script and start saying the first thing that came into her head, you get the picture. Although I have a lot of respect for her.

So under 'New Labour', all MPs were told they have to stick to the policies that came out of Milbank to the letter. This worked for a while and 'New Labour' came across as coherent and very electable. It worked.

Now the press hated this, they felt they could only get stifled quotes, that it killed real political debate. Also, to their credit, a lot of Labour MPs hated it, they felt straight jacketed by the whole thing. After a while, with so many complaints from all sides about it, it was abandoned, but it certainly changed the way people felt about the Labour Party. They were a serious party ready for Government.

Now back to my course. Before we attended, we were given a pamphlet on the course content. There were two things that really stuck in my mind. One, if the press gets in touch with you, normally by mobile phone, you ask what it's about, tell them you can't speak right now as you're just about to go into a meeting, research the subject thoroughly and get back to them. Two, never wear a striped shirt with a stripy tie on television, they just start blurring each other out. It looks like they're moving on the camera; you end up looking at the shirt and tie and not listening to what is being said. They're two good lessons in life.

Anyway, the tutor asks in a real powerful way, "What should you do if the press contacts you by phone?". I put my hand up and give the answer that I had read in her pamphlet. This threw her and she stumbled for a split-second and then said, "Perfect answer". So, I casually said "Yeah, I read your pamphlet", and everyone, including the tutor, laughed.

Now back to Nigel Farage, the whole point of this story. His mother lived next door to me, when I lived in Downe Village in Kent. He would often be seen and heard in our local pubs, giving his omnibus speeches. Saying, or rather pandering, to what everyone is saying in all public places all over the county at any given time. "We want our fishing rights back", "No more immigrants", "Send 'em all home". I do not wish to be political right now, but I'm always very sceptical of politicians who can identify problems but cannot articulate the answers.

But one cannot deny the success Nigel Farage is having, he has become quite a polished politician. But he used to be a city boy and always wore striped shirts and a striped tie and in the early days suffered from not being properly prepared for interviews.

I gave his mum a copy of this media training pamphlet and said Nigel might like to read this. I cannot claim to be, or would want to be, a part of his success but after I gave his mother the pamphlet, he never wore a striped shirt on television again and was always prepared for interviews.

~ There's no such thing as a coincidence. Think about the big things in your life, you didn't plan it, you didn't plan to be there it happened to you. ~

Foxes

Three little stories about Foxes.

I was eighteen years old; I had passed my driving test and was the proud owner of a Ford Capri. I thought this car was really special. Doyle drove one in 'The Professionals', a hit series on television at the time. To me it was a Ferrari. And I always carried a shovel in the boot.

I was boxing at the time and got loads of work digging footings for building sites. This was before small mechanical diggers had been invented. I would earn fifty pounds a day digging, this was good money then. I was given a labourer, to run the wheelbarrow, and a skip. I could usually get it filled by two o'clock and go home. But the main reason I did it was it was such good body conditioning. If you dig, your hands, shoulders and stomach muscles would be rock hard. It's the best training you can get, better than anything you could do in a gym.

So, one evening I'm driving home from somewhere late in the dark and I go over the brow of a hill. I see these two lights shining at me from the middle of the road and I hear a 'donk' from underneath my car as I drive over it. It came at me too late to brake. I pulled up to see what it was and I had hit a fox. The poor bugger was screaming in pain. If you have ever heard a fox in pain it sounds like a little girl screaming. It was horrible. I knew I couldn't just leave it there screaming, so I went and got my shovel out of the boot and hit it across the head as hard as I could. The thing is I didn't kill it. I wanted to put it out of its pain, but all I actually did was make it scream even more. I felt awful. I knew I couldn't hit it again, I wouldn't have been able to do it, so I picked it up and put it in the boot of my car.

I drove to a vet I knew in Bromley and woke them up; they were really kind and took it off me and thanked me for bringing it to them. I didn't tell them that after I had hit it with my car, I then hit it with a shovel.

Anyway, the next day I rang them up to find out what had happened to it. I expected them to say, "Oh it died in the night". But they didn't, they said it was fine this morning, so they had released it.

1987, I'm really cracking on, big house in Bromley, worth loads of money, living the dream in Maggie's Britain. Nobody warned me that interest rates were going to triple, there'll be a property crash, and I would lose everything. That sure came as a surprise. Thanks Maggie. 'Kiss my arse'.

Anyway, after I had lost everything and was living back at home, Neil, a friend of mine, had seen this house in Farnbourgh Village and basically made me buy it. I knew he was right and went along with him, glad he was there actually. The thing was, I was back where I started five years ago; living in a shithole, working on a rundown house, trying to turn it into a home, having lost the lot last time. I felt like a bit part in Rudyard Kipling's 'If'.

> *'Or watch the things you gave your life to, broken*
>
> *And stoop and build them up with worn out tools.'*

So, I'm sleeping on a camp bed next to a load of bags of cement and get up to make a coffee and start work. As I get to the kitchen, this fox pops his head around the door. The back of the house was all open. The poor bastard froze but he had nowhere to go. His front leg was obviously broken; his tail was all twisted, and its coat was a mess. He must have answered to the name of lucky. It looked at me. I just said, "Don't worry son" and looked in the fridge. There was only one egg, but I cracked it into a saucer, and it larruped it up. When it had finished it, it looked up, and if a fox can say 'thank you' through its eyes it said it. I said, "Don't worry son, I know how you feel" and it went on its way.

At the back of my mum's flat there was a fox's den. A whole family lived there, and every morning my mum would throw them out a chicken sandwich. She would cut them into triangles to throw at them, and they would line up in the garden to get them. I asked her once, "Why don't you just throw the bread and the chicken out the window; they will still eat it all". She said, "Ah they like a sandwich". But the most amazing thing was, she buttered the bread.

~ Talks cheap money buys houses. ~

I must go down to the seas again, to the lonely sea and the sky,

And all I ask is a tall ship and a star to steer her by;

And the wheel's kick and the wind's song and the white sail's shaking,

And a grey mist on the sea's face, and a grey dawn breaking.

I must go down to the seas again, for the call of the running tide

Is a wild call and a clear call that may not be denied;

And all I ask is a windy day with the white clouds flying,

And the flung spray and the blown spume, and the seagulls crying.

I must go down to the seas again, to the vagrant gypsy life,

To the gull's way and the whale's way where the wind's like a whetted knife;

And all I ask is a merry yarn from a laughing fellow-rover,

And quiet sleep and a sweet dream when the long trick's over.

- John Masefeild

Anyway, that's your lot, thanks for reading, take care.

Brendan.

Printed in Dunstable, United Kingdom

74336550R00109